❧ *By John Hall Wheelock*

WHAT IS POETRY?
THE GARDENER AND OTHER POEMS
POEMS OLD AND NEW
POEMS, 1911–1936
THE BRIGHT DOOM
THE BLACK PANTHER
DUST AND LIGHT
LOVE AND LIBERATION
THE BELOVÈD ADVENTURE
THE HUMAN FANTASY

❧❧ *Selected and Edited by,*
with Introduction

POETS OF TODAY VIII
POETS OF TODAY VII
POETS OF TODAY VI
POETS OF TODAY V
POETS OF TODAY IV
POETS OF TODAY III
POETS OF TODAY II
POETS OF TODAY I
EDITOR TO AUTHOR:
The Letters of Maxwell E. Perkins
THE FACE OF A NATION: *Poetical Passages*
from the Writings of Thomas Wolfe

WHAT IS POETRY?

WHAT IS POETRY?

By John Hall Wheelock

Charles Scribner's Sons · NEW YORK

Library of Congress Catalog Card Number 63-14034

❧ Habit, routine, our daily humdrum apathy and indifference, this is the shield we put between us and reality, the shield with which we protect ourselves from life while we are engaged in the business of living. It is the function of the arts to pierce that shield, to re-awaken in us a forgotten knowledge.

To CHARLES SCRIBNER

⋱ *Preface*

The greater part of the material here included has appeared in the form of introductory essays to the volumes, published between 1954 and 1960, in the *Poets Of Today* series. For the purposes of this book, new material has been added, and there has been a good deal of cutting and revision in the interests of unity. It has not always been possible, however, to eliminate repetition and overlapping in the case of work derived from such disparate essays. Where occasional repetitive passages were inextricably involved in matter essential to the main theme of the essay, they have been allowed to stand.

Some of the chapters in this volume, or the greater part of them, were first published in periodicals, as follows: "Poetry and Prose, the Essential Difference" and "A True Poem Is a Way of Knowing," in *The New York Times Book Review;* "To Recapture Delight," in *The American Scholar,* under the title, "A

View of Contemporary Poetry"; "The Process and the Poem," in *Partisan Review,* under the title, "Putting Salt on the Tail of a Poem"; and "Some Thoughts on Poetry," in *The Arizona Quarterly.*

The greater portion of "On a Certain Resistance" was part of a lecture, "The Two Knowledges: An Essay on a Certain Resistance," delivered on January 27, 1958, at The Library of Congress, under the auspices of The Gertrude Clarke Whittall Poetry and Literature Fund, and later published by The Library of Congress. It served also, under the same title, as the basis for the William Vaughn Moody Lecture, delivered on November 27, 1962, at the University of Chicago.

The quotations from T. S. Eliot in Chapter III, "The Fourth Voice of Poetry," are reprinted, by permission of Mr. Eliot, from his *The Three Voices of Poetry,* copyright, 1953, by Cambridge University Press.

Grateful acknowledgment is made to all the above, and to Mr. Allen Tate for my indebtedness, in much, to his *The Man of Letters in the Modern World.* For helpful criticism and suggestions in connection with Chapter VI, "On a Certain Resistance," I wish especially to thank Mr. Charles Scribner.

J. H. W.

April, 1963

[xii]

ᴇ§ *Contents*

[xiii]

WHAT IS POETRY?

1

POETRY AND PROSE,
THE ESSENTIAL DIFFERENCE

What is poetry? What is prose? Is there any way of defining the essential difference between the two categories into which we have divided literature? It is the more obvious difference, the difference in form, that gets us off to a wrong start. As the school-boy said, "Poetry is written in verse; prose is written in plain English". Yet, certainly, the difference in form is not the essential difference. There are passages in the King James version of the Bible that can't be cast out of the category of poetry merely because they are written in prose. Yeats opens *The Oxford Book of Modern Verse* with a passage from Walter Pater. The prose poem is an accepted, if momentarily unfashionable, genre. The verse, on the other hand, that comes to you over the radio celebrating the virtues of a breakfast food, will not, for all its rhyme and rhythm, fit into any conceivable definition of poetry.

The matter of rhythm, incidentally, has sometimes been claimed as the determining factor in distinguishing what is poetry from what is prose. In the former, according to this criterion, the rhythms will be more regular, more recurrent; in the latter they will have greater variety and complexity. But the facts do not always bear this out. Impassioned rhetorical prose—a Fourth of July oration, for instance (surely, the direct antithesis to poetry)—tends to fall into iambic pentameter almost metronomic in its regularity. The skilled poet, however, varies his stresses within the fixed measure, and in poetry employing free cadence, in vers libre, and in poetry as practiced by Ossian, by Whitman, by Jeffers, and how many others, the rhythms are as varied and as irregular as they are in prose.

It's all very confusing. Verse is often "prosy", and bad prose may be, and usually is, "poetic". Note that we can refer to bad poetry as "verse", but that, in the case of prose, as Mr. Eliot has pointed out, we have no word to distinguish the worst from the best. A still further confusion arises from the ambiguity of the word "verse". It may designate the form that poetry customarily takes, or, though less often, the mere form without the spirit. Is, then, the difference between poetry and prose a difference of spirit? When we consider the enormous range of mood and approach to be found in both, it becomes clear that this is not the answer.

Perhaps a definition of poetry itself will give us some clue to the essential difference between poetry and prose. There are almost as many of these definitions as there are poets, and possibly the best, as well as the briefest, is Frost's apt and mischievous bon mot: "Poetry is what gets lost in translation." Why is this so? Isn't it possible to translate the ideas conveyed in a poem? Yes. And the feelings it expresses? Certainly. But, as Mallarmé has told us, a poem is not made of ideas or of feelings, but of words. You cannot translate the words of a poem in such a way as to translate their meaning and yet reproduce their original rhythm and color, their identical associative and aural values, all those nuances of sound and of symbolism that are a poem's very essence. Moreover, the syntactical order in which words are arranged varies from language to language, and the over-all effect of the words in the original may not be preserved when they are re-arranged in the order imposed upon them by translation. Also, there are words in each language that have no equivalent in another. The French have no word for "home"; there is no verb in English that is the exact counterpart of the

German verb, "lauschen", nor does the German "gucken" adequately render the implications of the English verb, "to peer".

Once we grasp the tremendously important rôle that words play in poetry, as compared to the rôle they play in prose, it may help us to a definition of the difference between the two categories. A poem will result when the genius of a language—its words, their sound and their sense—offers the genius of a poet an opportunity to perform a miracle. That masterpiece of coincidence, that achieved miracle, the poem, with its unique syllabic patterns, its unique consonantal and vowel music, its seemingly inevitable cadences (partly the result of skill, partly the result of sheer good luck), is not translatable. The differing genius of every language makes this impossible. No one has yet succeeded in translating into English poetry Heine's famous line, "Du bist wie eine Blume". It is translated into prose only when we say, "You are like a flower".

Are we not now ready to make an attempt at defining, however loosely, the essential difference between poetry and prose? Nothing in nature, or in art, can, of course, be delimited with absolute exactitude. Perhaps we can put it this way: <u>In poetry, words are employed more as an end, and less as a means merely, than is the case in prose.</u>

~§ 2

A TRUE POEM
IS A WAY OF KNOWING

Poetry strips the veil of familiarity from things.

SHELLEY

~§   As Kenneth Burke has said, man is "specifically the symbol-using animal". Language is not only
his greatest single source of happiness, it is his most
important invention. Language implies collaboration
in symbolism. So simple a thing as a word, by general consent symbolizes, or stands for, an infinitely
manifold, infinitely complex, item of experience. A
poem is a constellation of such symbols, representing
a poet's re-discovery of some phase of reality. By
dealing with things, by making use of them, by
becoming accustomed to them, as we say, we lose
sight of them. Most of us pass through life in a state
of semi-anaesthesia. The world about us has become

[21]

so familiar that we no longer experience it. It is not sufficient that things be apprehended or the idea of them intellectually conveyed. If we are to re-experience them, they must be revealed anew. Poetry, like all the arts, is revelation. A poem gives the world back to the maker of the poem, in all its original strangeness, the shock of its first surprise. It is capable of doing the same for the rest of us.

The charge most frequently brought against the contemporary poem is the charge of obscurity. Should not a poem be clear? So naive a question can best be answered by another equally frank: Clear to whom? A poem is a way of knowing and feeling that requires, for its understanding, a modicum of imagination, and some familiarity with the conventions of the art. There are persons to whom the verse of Robert Louis Stevenson must remain enigmatic. The lines from Tennyson, "Alone and warming his five wits/ The white owl in the belfry sits", struck, one may recall, Yeats's literal-minded acquaintance as "the observation of a lunatic". So with Omar Khayyam's "I came like water, and like wind I go". "What is the meaning of that?" he inquired. "How is that possible—'I came like water, and like wind I go'?" This was an extreme case, no doubt, but there are such people. Their point-of-view, as contrasted with that of a poet, is summed up in the classic stanza by

Franklin P. Adams: "I see the business office,/ And I see the floor above it./ I see and hear a lot of things./ Suppose I do. What of it?" To the reader capable of enjoying poetry, and familiar with it, the fully achieved work of the sincere poets of our day, even when they are innovators, will be as clear as any poem is called upon to be—clear, that is, after thoughtful re-readings, the gradual living oneself into it, that new and complex work may exact.

That there are exceptions, contemporary poems that remain obscure, even to the qualified reader, and after long familiarity, must be admitted. Such obscurity may have its origin in the intrinsic abstrusity of the material with which the poem grapples. A poem may take a generation to yield its full secret. One might even say that a poem's meaning varies from age to age, since though fixed in its outer form as originally established, it has an existence in the public mind, and develops there like a living thing. Then, there are the cases where the difficulty lies in the inadequacy of the reader's equipment. The many learnèd allusions that run through "Paradise Lost", for instance, meant little at the time to the average reader and mean even less to most of us today, for they assume a knowledge that was not and is not general. In that sense, an abstract poem by Wallace Stevens, shall we say, is no more obscure than is "The Phoenix and the Turtle", though for reasons other than those that made and make the latter so difficult. Both require, for their interpretation, an equipment beyond that which the reader is likely to possess. But, more often, obscurity results from failure on the part of the poet to consummate his intention. It may sometimes occur through the mere omission of clues essential to understanding, as when a humorous story is told without the data necessary to its point. Too much has been taken for granted, a common fault of the imagination.

Certain contemporary poets, however, in revolt perhaps against the tedium of the mass mind, have cast off "vulgar intelligibility". They would be armored against understanding, and if obscurity and paraded erudition will serve, the more obscure and the more erudite the better. They have gone beyond even Goethe's uncharacteristically craven advice in his *West-östlicher Diwan*, ("Sagt es niemand, nur den Weisen,/ Weil die Menge gleich verhöhnet"— "Don't tell it to anyone except the initiated, because the multitude will only jeer at you"), and would keep every one in the dark, including themselves. What could be worse than to be rejected by the reader? they ask. Why, only one thing, of course—to be accepted by him. And their efforts to forestall this are often successful, resulting in achievements that baffle even the hardened addict of hermetic verse. But we are not here concerned with poems that fail to make their point, either unintentionally or with "malice prepense". The former are innocent failures, the product of sincerity, industry, and application where, to use a phrase of Richard Wagner's, "nothing is lacking except talent". The gruesome specimens in the latter category, on the other hand, are the product, occasionally, of a very real talent misdirected and ill advised.

A charge less often, and more justly, brought than that of obscurity will be the complaint that the contemporary poem is cerebral, accomplished, erudite, and empty of feeling. If Wordsworth were alive today, he might be tempted to change his rather unsatisfactory definition of poetry to "emotion recollected in anxiety and with distaste". Somewhere, in too many a contemporary poem, between the impulse of feeling and its manifestation a Freudian "censor" has intervened. Emotion is not permitted to get through except in disguise, wit being the mask most favored for this purpose. Our age, like the Augustan age of Queen Anne, is ashamed and afraid of emotion. A poet is praised for being "tough"— "a tough thinker", "a tough-minded lyricist"—though just what he's supposed to be so tough about it's hard to determine. But the censorship with regard to the expression of feeling is severe. And, indeed, in our time, any deviation, in the arts, from the taste prescribed must face criticism that is not aesthetic judgment so much as moral condemnation. The heretic is burned at the stake. It is as if the rigors of orthodoxy had been transferred from the religious to the aesthetic field.

Among the heresies most frowned upon is the theory and practice of poetry as an art predominantly aural. Swinburne's reference to Poe as "the only singing voice amid the numerous corn-crakes of American literature", from the point-of-view of current doctrine places the emphasis on the least important element of distinction. The old notion of "harmonious numbers" would get short shrift today. The break with the whole romantic tradition, the post-Swinburnian reaction against verbal virtuosity and the sonorous or even the melodious in verse, has initiated a swing to the opposite extreme. Verbal magic, the incantatory, even the lyrical have, with a few striking exceptions, given way to the didactic, the expository, the analytic; the music of words to the interplay of image and idea.

Another of the more reprehensible heresies is the concept of the poem as communication, and certainly though language, the prime medium of communication, is also the medium of poetry, the term is a very incomplete and, in some ways, misleading description. Communion, within a potentially universal fellowship, comes nearer the mark. A poem does not originate out of an impulse to communicate. A poem is what happens when a poet re-discovers, for himself, the reality we have lost sight of because, to use Shelley's metaphor, it has been overlaid by the veil of familiarity. The process, however, is not one of re-discovery and subsequent transmittal in a poem. The poem itself is part of the re-discovery. In making it, the poet learns what it is that he has re-discovered. Thus a child, when it begins to speak, learns what it is that it knows. And as a child will talk to itself, with no one around to hear, so in the poem the poet, it might be said, is talking to himself. He has established communication with his own being, and therefore potentially with others. What was subject has become object. What was on the inside is now on the outside. It can be looked at and shared. The fact that, through language, this sharing can come to pass is proof of the identity of men, of their correspondences. Man is one Self. Those "others" are you.

The struggle of this Self with the world around it, the old contest between the ego and the universe, that unequal contest with its inevitable issue, has been the underlying theme in the work of every poet from Homer to Eliot. It is implicit in any poet's vision of reality. For poetry, like the other arts, gets its meaning from the tragic nature of things, whether as escape from it in play, or celebration of it in the more exalted moments. Against the backdrop of fate, life shows at its noblest and most endearing. Its glory is in its doom. The inexorable truth is the music to which all the arts move, in rage or delight, with proud or dancing step.

3

THE FOURTH VOICE OF POETRY

There are the lines, in a play by one of the
supreme poetic dramatists, in which we hear a
more impersonal voice still than that of either
the character or the author.

T. S. ELIOT

In his *The Situation of Poetry*, M. Maritain
touches a profound truth when he describes a poem
as a form of knowledge that is "not ordered to knowing but to being expressed in a work". Its aim, method
and end-result is the creation of a new thing. That
new thing represents a knowledge that could have
been realised in no other way. In a universe in which
everything has meaning, and in which all meanings
are related and symbolize one another, the poet lives
perpetually on the edge of discovery. As Walt Whitman said of himself, "I lie abstracted and hear

[29]

beautiful tales of things and the reasons of things,/
They are so beautiful I nudge myself to listen".

Yet not merely to listen. It is the poet's function
to understand, to interpret, to learn what it is he is
being told, by giving form to the formless, a body
to the bodiless something plucking at him: ". . .
bodiless childful of life in the gloom/ Crying with
frog voice, 'What shall I be?' "—these lines of
Beddoes are quoted by Mr. Eliot, in his *The Three
Voices of Poetry*, as applicable (though not so applied by Beddoes) to the dark ghost of the poem as
yet unborn. With the taking on of form, however
rudimentary at first (a process the poet must be careful not to inhibit by trying to hurry or force it, or by
concentrating on it too intently), a little miracle has
occurred. For the poet's initial dilemma might have
been summed up in a couplet: "How shall I find a
body for the thought I haven't got?/ For unless it
have a body, there cannot be a thought." As the body
of the poem evolves, its meaning, what might be
called its thought, is revealed. An act of transub-
stantiation takes place. Words and rhythms have become an experience of a truth.

The statement of M. Maritain, quoted at the
beginning of this chapter, in which he describes a
poem as a form of knowledge "not ordered to knowing but to being expressed in a work", gives us the

clue. The poet, troubled by an awareness of something not fully understood, is impelled, implies Maritain, to the creation of a new thing that shall embody it and thus reveal it, to himself and, perhaps, to others. This new thing is the poem, a knowledge that without such embodiment would have remained a vague tantalization, an uncomfortable secret at the edge of consciousness. That there are, in every age, men and women compelled, one might say, to take upon themselves, in the face of all the ordinary other and quite sufficient difficulties of life, a task so thankless and so nearly impossible as that of giving a body to the bodiless essence of things, is proof of the almost obsessive power that the mystery of experience has over the human spirit. The mystery in which we are placed torments us; the making of a poem is a bit of research, an effort to understand, a form of assuagement.

It is impossible to get at the secret of poetry by the analytic method, "untwisting all the chains that tie/ The hidden soul of harmony". Yet analysis will yield data of importance. Relationships and distinctions may be uncovered, an awareness of which will enhance our understanding and our enjoyment. In his *The Three Voices of Poetry,* already referred to, Mr. Eliot makes one of the most interesting and useful of such distinctions.

The "three voices", according to Mr. Eliot, may be defined as follows: "The voice of the poet talking to himself—or to nobody . . . directly expressing the poet's own thoughts and sentiments"; "the voice of the poet addressing an audience, whether large or small", in "poetry intended to amuse or instruct, poetry that tells a story, poetry that preaches or points a moral"; and, lastly, "the voice of the poet when he attempts to create a dramatic character speaking in verse; when he is saying, not what he would say in his own person, but only what he can say within the limits of one imaginary character addressing another imaginary character". Eliot makes it clear that these distinctions are tentative: there could be fewer or still other categories. He points out, moreover, that the three voices are not "mutually exclusive", but are often found together—the first and second in non-dramatic poetry, and "together with the third in dramatic poetry too", that there you will sometimes hear the voice of the author and the voice of his character speaking as one voice. "Finally", Eliot goes on to say, "there are the lines, in a play by one of the supreme poetic dramatists, in which we hear a more impersonal voice still than that of either the character or the author".

May one not suggest, as an addition to the tentative three categories already enumerated, that of a fourth voice, not "the voice of the poet talking to himself—or to nobody", nor "addressing an audience, whether large or small", nor speaking through a dramatic character and not for himself, but a voice, not his own, the "more impersonal voice" referred to above, speaking through him, in the great moments of unconscious divination, out of some older, wiser Self in which all selves are included? Where this fourth voice is speaking—and it may be heard in unison with any one of the other three, or all four may be sounding together—you have everything that is most memorable in poetry.

It can be argued that, while it is a simple matter to know when one of the first three voices is speaking, associated as each is with a distinct kind of poem, the presence or absence of the fourth voice will be a matter of opinion, and that the category is therefore a purely fanciful one. And yet there are lines and passages, in poems of every description, that readers of varying degrees of perceptivity, different points of view and opposite temperaments, have almost unanimously singled out, over the generations, despite all the changes in literary taste and fashion, as especially noteworthy—lines where a voice, not the poet's, yet issuing from him, speaks with an authority and a finality that compel acceptance. These are the lines and passages that, intuition tells us, have not been invented so much as discovered. Like the great passages in music, a theme of Bach's, a melody of Beethoven's, they seem to have existed forever, regardless of whatever point in time may have marked the moment of their revelation here, their sudden sounding forth, as it were, out of some other world in which they have their being.

Every reader will summon to memory, readily enough, examples or instances where what we may term the fourth voice is speaking. The plays of Shakespeare abound, of course, in such examples. One thinks of the famous passage beginning "To-morrow, and tomorrow, and tomorrow", and of the lines, "We are such stuff/ As dreams are made on, and our little life/ Is rounded with a sleep". The voice is heard in Dante's "e la sua volontate è nostra pace"; in Goethe, in his Prologue to *Faust*, in the exultant "Die unbeschreiblich hohen Werke/ Sind herrlich wie am ersten Tag"; in Wordsworth's "Our birth is but a sleep and a forgetting:/ The soul that rises with us, our life's star,/ Hath had elsewhere its setting". It is clear in the startling simplicity of Coleridge's "He prayeth best, who loveth best/ All things both great and small", and in the equally startling strangeness of Marvell's "But at my back I always hear/ Time's wingèd chariot hurrying near", or of Yeats's "A starlit or a moonlit dome disdains/

All that man is,/ All mere complexities,/ The fury and the mire of human veins". Keats, through an intense self-discipline and a consecration amounting to an act of prayer, made of himself so effective and selfless an instrument for the great moods of poetry, that many of his poems are like mosaics composed of those timeless passages through which the fourth voice echoes and reverberates: "When old age shall this generation waste,/ Thou shalt remain, in midst of other woe/ Than ours"; "Heard melodies are sweet but those unheard/ Are sweeter"; "A sun— a shadow of a magnitude"/—these bear Keats's own accent, but what is speaking through them sounds overtones not his own.

Again, what we have called the fourth voice will sometimes reveal itself in a depth of perception, where human emotions are concerned, that seems, in a flash, to lay bare the very roots of feeling. A brief statement, when this voice is speaking, may sum up unutterable things, as in Lear's cry, "Pity me, but do not speak to me", or when the dying Hamlet says to Horatio, "If thou did'st ever hold me in thy heart,/ Absent thee from felicity awhile/ And in this harsh world draw thy breath in pain". The poignance of that voice becomes almost unbearable in the stark compression of Wilfrid Owen's line, "I am the enemy you killed, my friend". One hears it in the strange aptness of Shelley's "Bright reason will mock thee/ Like the sun from a wintry sky".

But more often the fourth voice is discernible in the character of its expression, in a way of saying what may not, in itself, be of intrinsic importance— in unforgettable description, beyond the reach of conscious artifice, magical evocation of the thing to be re-experienced. Wordsworth has become its medium when he tells us that "The moon doth with delight/ Look round her when the heavens are bare"; Blake, when he gives us "The lost traveller's dream under the hill". It speaks with the accent of Milton in "By slow Meander's margent green,/ Or by the violet-embroidered vale"; of Addison, in his "The spangled heavens, a shining frame". Other classical examples would certainly include the passage, in Keats's last sonnet, where, in two lines, the sense of planetary ocean, what the Germans call *das Weltmeer*, is instantaneously conveyed, "The moving waters at their priestlike task/ Of pure ablution round earth's human shores". The same magic is felt in lines by poets as opposite as Eliot when he writes, "Yet there the nightingale/ Filled all the desert with inviolable voice", and Swinburne, with his "The immeasurable tremor of all the sea".

The examples given above have, in each case, the unmistakable tone and manner of the author quoted, but with something over and beyond what

is characteristic, a finality, a perfection, occurring
only now and again, as if, at such times, in a
moment of selflessness, the poet had become an instrument through which another, profounder, less
personal, voice was speaking.

Whose, then, is this voice that we have termed
the fourth voice—the voice least often sounding in
any poem, and in any poem the voice carrying
farthest, best heard by the many, and the longest
remembered? If we say it is the voice of the unconscious in each one of us, or if we say it is the
voice of the race, we are saying much the same
thing. The unconscious, as Jung has suggested, may
be likened to an ocean, of which all individual con-
sciousnesses are the inlets. Like the ocean it is
wary of giving up its secrets. It is, for the most part,
silent. When it speaks, it is as if it spoke *from* all
of us *to* all of us. In any poem, long or short, the
actual poetry, as Poe implied, is in the passages
where this unconscious power has been at work,
passages that seemed, to the poet, almost to write
themselves. These are held together by the necessary
connective tissue between them. To weave the connective tissue so skilfully that it will not make too
painful a contrast with the passages that wrote themselves—this, Edwin Arlington Robinson used to
say, is the test of a poet's art and discipline.

Yet no art, however disciplined, can so order

words as to create the illusion of that seemingly accidental inevitability with which they fall into place when something beyond art is speaking. After all, words are not playthings; in the highest sense, they are not even tools, but the outward evidence of an inner reality. The visitations of what we have called the fourth voice of poetry are not to be commanded. Certainly, it is the voice for which every poet waits. The long, lonely labor and self-discipline are his prayer that he may be an instrument worthy of that voice if it should come, to speak through him the words and the wisdom that are somehow beyond his own scope and clairvoyance. It is this conjunction of almost more than mortal longing and the stars that alone makes possible the transcendent revelation.

✑ 4

THE POEM
IN THE NUCLEAR AGE

We must love one another or die.

AUDEN

✑   "... When I speak to you about myself, I am speaking to you about yourself. How is it you don't see that?" In these words Victor Hugo puts his finger on the secret behind all communication. For if it is the separation into selves that makes communication necessary, it is their basic oneness that makes it possible. Whether by the use of words, or, as in the case of bees, by means of symbolic acts and precision dances, communication predicates a prior mutual agreement resting upon the correspondences between selves that, though separate, at root are one. Language is such a prior mutual agreement, one of the forms through which the "I-Thou", to borrow

[39]

Martin Buber's phrase, expresses itself. In a world where the sole relationship was the "I-It", there would be no need for, or possibility of, language. Swinburne, himself not notable for any lack of eloquence, has written ". . . words divide and rend;/ But silence is most noble till the end." Actually, of course—and who knew it better than he did!—words are symbols of the unity existing throughout the parts of one multitudinous Self, divided in this very way, perhaps, in order to effect the maximum opportunity for communication, as a tree puts forth its multiplicity of leaves, which talk to one another when the wind moves among them.

Communication, then, in the deepest sense, is soliloquy reverberating through a complex of related selves. Hugo was right, and Karl Shapiro is right in his feeling, expressed somewhere in *Beyond Criticism*, that the poem, the form of language that tries to say the unsayable, to suggest by rhythm, cadence and structure what cannot be put into words, is not communication as we ordinarily understand it. Where expression is spontaneous and that which is expressed comes from depths common to all, what we term communication will take place spontaneously. Obviously, the more inclusive and the more definite the area of understanding that is shared, the more complete will be the interaction between us. The fact that we all are human beings, involved in the same drama of birth, life, and death—this constitutes our primary mutual system of reference. A common race or culture, beliefs, mythologies and legends held in common, and the understandings and prior meeting of minds that these imply, still further heighten rapport. When a poet, using these, speaks out of the impulse of his heart, images, ideas and emotions very closely corresponding to his own are evoked in the hearts of those who are at one with him in sharing the same heritage. If you have ever listened to the talk of baseball fans, or even of Income Tax experts (for the Income Tax, in all its refinements, has become an art form), you will realize how much of what we call communication is pure soliloquy based upon a mutual system of reference—in other words, upon a prior unity of minds.

The poet is enabled to arouse the fullest response, and the one most nearly identical with his own excitement, by the use of allusions, legends, myths or beliefs, familiar to his readers, or listeners. Dante and Milton, as Yeats points out, had their mythologies; Shakespeare, the characters of English history and of traditional romance. These had well defined connotations for a large number of people. In our own day, we have experienced an enormous increase in the means of communication, but with this increase there has come about a steady decrease in the body of myth, legend and belief familiar to all—a familiarity that had made possible, in poetry and the other arts, the total response that can be called forth only where artist and public have roots in the same cultural soil. To cite an example on the most elementary level, if you have never heard of Cain, the phrase, "the curse of Cain", will be meaningless. On a more complex level, if you haven't read Wordsworth, you will make little sense of Housman's mischievous lines, "O cuckoo, shall I call thee bird/ Or but a wandering voice?/ State the alternative preferred,/ With reasons for your choice."

In the same way, the unseen connections in words themselves, the auras around them, so important in a poem, have today in many cases been lost. It would be difficult indeed to make a poem out of scientific terminology, out of words unhallowed as yet by overtones and auras of association. The poet who attempts it, under such a title, for instance, as "A History of the Universe from the Point-of-View of the Organization of Matter", is taking upon himself a task unnecessarily difficult and unrewarding. If the line from Eliot, "I gotta use words when I talk to you", describes the implements of the poet, the poet must know better than to think that mere precision tools will serve. He may dispute this, asserting that the language of science, because of its freedom from prior associations, is the ideal language for the "new poetry". But he will be as wrong as was the young woman who attributed to Walt Whitman the remark: "As for living, our servants will do that for us."

With the disappearance of the public mythologies, certain poets have felt obliged to invent private ones —and this, of course, makes exegesis, in the form of critical apparatus and notes, necessary. There has, perhaps, seldom been a time, as far as poetry in the English tongue is concerned, where so much work of a high order has been achieved as during the first half of the twentieth century. That there has been, also, a large output of verse so obscure and pedantic as to establish slight contact between poet and reader may be ascribed to three factors: the use of a private mythology, private semantics, and the purely erudite or critical approach. The temper of the age, like that of the eighteenth century, has become predominantly critical. Tolstoi's remark, that "it isn't sufficient to be stupid, one must be well read also", is applicable today, if for the word "stupid" you substitute "unperceptive". Critics swarm and, like the white mice of the laboratory, having consumed whatever supply of pabulum lies within reach, begin devouring one another. In the presence of so many poems sired by erudition upon industriousness, one longs—to paraphrase a witticism of Yeats's*—for that imaginary book with real poems in it. The actual book with which one is confronted is sometimes all too real. Then it will almost seem as if it is only birds that sing spontaneously and by ear—though not without notes, some wag might add. Footnotes probably.

A private mythology or system of reference, private semantics, and an over-ballast of erudition as against feeling are, we have found, the commonest causes of much that is obscure in the kind of poem we have been discussing. Robert Frost has said that "two fears should follow us through life: the fear that we shan't prove worthy in the eyes of someone who knows us at least as well as we know ourselves (which is the fear of God); and then, the fear of man, the fear that men won't understand us and we shall be cut off from them." Is the contemporary cleft in the unity of man, in the very basis of his communion with himself—this sometimes seemingly wilful disregard of the I-Thou, so prevalent today—a symptom of our disastrous half-century or, more ominously, of some approaching disintegration?

In the nuclear age, nature through the agency of man, who is a part of nature, has acquired the power to commit suicide. It is reasonable and, even if it

* See his *Ideas of Good and Evil*, "imaginary gardens with real toads in them".

wasn't, it is necessary to believe that this will not take place, that the intelligence that brought this potentiality into being will be able to control it, and that mankind, of sheer necessity, will become more unified than it has ever been. Evolution, which produced them, has proved the survival value of the social and co-operative virtues. They are now revealed as more essential, at this stage of history, than the aggressive and competitive instincts. The nuclear age emphasizes this. To quote Auden: "We must love one another or die." And "love", a slippery word, must include not only "Gentleness, virtue, wisdom and endurance", but strength. It must not run the risk implied by Dr. Niebuhr when he says: "Love without power is an invitation to surrender the world to power without love." The closer unity and community among men that must ensue will make possible a literature greater and more widely shared than ever before, a communion profounder and more meaningful than ever before.

Above all, the nuclear age dramatizes and brings home to us, with almost blinding vividness, the fact of our mortality—not simply the mortality of the individual but of the race. Whether extinction comes as a result of a gradual process, of a cosmic accident, or of his own unbridled tensions, man will not be eternal on this planet; the planet itself will not last forever. We are thereby instructed, once and for all, that the final values are not material and quantitative —mere mass, force and duration—but spiritual and qualitative. The bit of brief consciousness that can take in the sweep of the galaxy—adding, in the creative merging of subject and object, its truth and beauty and meaning to the brute swarms of matter orbiting through space—in the end, outweighs them all. The poem, in the nuclear age, will reveal a more immediate sense of the secret behind the tragic flux.

~§ 5

TO RECAPTURE DELIGHT

Delight is the chief, if not the only, end of poetry.
DRYDEN

~§ The key to the tragic nature of things is the division into selves. Conscious being becomes possible only in a self, yet to be a self means to be capable of pain as well as of pleasure, and brings with it the ultimate penalty of death. Moreover, the very fact of selfhood implies separation, implies a clash of interests. Just as two bodies cannot occupy the same space at the same moment, so the desires, even the needs, of selves often collide. Suffering is, therefore, of the essence of being. The self is self-ish, and in its selfishness, so requisite for individual survival, is at odds with another, greater, multitudinous entity, the non-self. We find the primal expression of this dichotomy in the preying of life upon life, the biological

[47]

necessity to which man, in common with many other animals, is subject. This conflict is further exemplified in the competitive struggle between men, whether in war or in so-called peace. Religion attempts to find a solution on the human level. Christianity, the religion of the West, finds the answer in the love that expresses itself in self-sacrifice. Christ on the Cross symbolizes, among other things, the reconciliation between self and non-self through a supreme act of self-sacrificing love. Love restores, in some measure, the unity broken by the division into selves.

But there is, apart from religion and the solution it offers, another area in which human selves are reconciled, in which the essential unity of man is revealed. Art—be it music, drama, painting, sculpture or poetry—a realm standing beyond and above the arena of the biological struggle, reveals it. For as the possibility of mere communication between men is, of itself, evidence of some underlying unity, so their capability of profound communion with one another, and with the collective unconscious, through a work of art, is proof of it. We have now reached a stage in history where recognition of this oneness becomes imperative. Man's cleverness has finally caught up with him. It is a truism that survival now depends on something much greater than cleverness: upon mutual good will, charity and co-operation, upon complete and effective realization that we are one.

Of all the arts, poetry, partly because its medium is the medium of everyday communication, partly because of its ability to convey, however indirectly, definite thoughts and feelings, has perhaps stood closest to man, been the most intimately expressive of his spiritual condition at any given time. With this in mind, it is interesting to examine some of the characteristics of poetry, in the English-speaking countries, during the past half-century, a period among the most violent and tragic in history and yet a period of amazing material progress and scientific achievement.

Whatever the "true tradition" in the poetry of the English-speaking peoples may be, whether it is in the line of those developments that reached their climax in the Romantic movement, as claimed by Sir Herbert Read, or in the line of the Metaphysicals and the Augustans, as generally believed by most contemporary critics, or whether, as Kathleen Raine has asserted, it comes down to us through Spenser, Milton, Blake, Wordsworth, Coleridge, and Yeats, one thing is certain: poetry took, during the first two decades of the twentieth century, a direction sharply divergent from that in its immediate past. The work of Ezra Pound and of T. S. Eliot, in criticism and in poetry, marked the beginning of a revolution, in both fields, whose influence was to be paramount during the rest of the half-century. And, again, whether the new direction taken was a desirable direction or in the line

[49]

of the "true tradition", or not, we may be sure that no amount of critical acumen could have foreseen or critical exhortation have changed it. Mr. Pound and Mr. Eliot, men of genius, through whose work French literature became once more the dominant influence in English poetry, were the voices of a point of view and a state of mind that had long been evolving and that were destined, under the pressures of the coming decades, to evolve still further in the same direction.

There are, of course, in any period, poets who are not representative of their time and who will constitute exceptions to any generalization made about it. Without regard to these, what may be described as the main characteristics distinguishing the poetry of the past fifty years from that which immediately preceded it? One thinks first, obviously, of the shift in tone and attitude that mark the break with the Romantic movement, of the rediscovery of Donne, with all his intricacies and complexities, and of the reaction against the virtues of such poets as Milton, Wordsworth, and Shelley. Looking more closely at the poems most representative of the period, one becomes aware to how large an extent perception has taken the place of emotion;* how much exact observation

* As Elizabeth Jennings has written, in a poem dealing with the post-Bomb generation's apparent inability to express feel-

and description there is and how little of the search for meaning—meaning that might have been derived from a synthesis of the isolated particulars so exactly observed and described. The point-of-view and the method are often those of science—analytic, precise, emotionally uninvolved. And the poem has grown more accurate and more learnèd,** sometimes to a point where the unravelling of allusions, references, and even of a private system of reference, has become the chief element of interest to many readers.

In his *Articulate Energy: An Inquiry into the Syntax of English Poetry*, Donald Davie discovers, throughout the poetry of our day, syntactical parallels to some of the characteristics we have been discussing. Much of the poetry of our time, he says, can be described as a poetry syntactically "invertebrate". And, certainly, it often is "a poetry . . . of vivid particularizations, of abrupt transitions, of ellipses, of inter-relations left implicit. . . . *The Waste Land* (or at least the end of it) and Mr. Ezra Pound's *Cantos* are poems which evoke vivid and precise isolated images, and on the whole leave it to the reader to establish

---

ing: "We only move it through the mind . . ./ Perhaps the deeper tragedy/ Is then the inability/ To change a thought into emotion."

** There is a taste for oddities, for abstruse data, from natural history and elsewhere, such as that the shark is the only fish that has eyelids, that snakes do not perspire, etc.

connections between these".* This kind of syntactical structure, the exact opposite of that to be found in the poetry of Milton, for instance, accounts for the absence, in most contemporary verse, of an over-all music, the flow of linkèd cadences long drawn out, with their rise and fall, their unresolved harmonies and suspended closes. For, as Susanne Langer, in her *Feeling and Form*, points out, it is as music, rather than as language, that poetry is held together by syntax. The aural pattern of much modern poetry is, by reason of its syntactical structure, necessarily, disjointed, episodic and staccato, as in the case of much modern music.

The characteristics we have touched upon as among those that are representative of the poetry of the past fifty years express the temper and mood of a period during which science has undermined many so-called truths, many cherished beliefs. The discoveries of Einstein and the physicists, no less than the theories of Freud and Jung, were fascinating but unsettling. Upheavals and disruptions, on a world scale, still further heightened the general bewilderment and disillusion. In the state of shock that followed these and their revelation of the brute potentialities in human nature, the idea of progress, of the perfecti-

* "The Poetic Skeleton" (a review of Dr. Davie's *Articulate Energy*), *The Times Literary Supplement*, November 4, 1955.

bility of man, of his innate goodness, suffered a set-back. There was a return to the psychology of the Middle Ages, to the concepts of original sin and other-worldly salvation. In poetry, the exhaustion conse-quent upon a surfeit of feeling was registered in a profound mistrust of feeling itself (unless masked as wit), in a cynical revulsion against the "falsity" of sentiment, and in a hearty dislike of the "grandiose" and harmonious verbal music of the Victorians. A bitter but "honest" dissonance was now preferred. In the same way, the scepticism engendered by the collapse of familiar ideals and ideologies expressed itself in a mistrust of *all* meaning. The poetic impulse rested, and took refuge in accurate, objective record-ing of the report of the senses, unvitiated by emotion or reflection. The awareness of totality was lost.

Throughout this period, which embraced two world wars and a major depression, the poem, as prac-tised by the English-speaking peoples, showed, never-theless, an extraordinary creativity and versatility. While originality in the arts customarily rests upon the nuances that distinguish one individual from another rather than upon drastic formal innovation, the poetry of the past half century has, undeniably, been enriched by radical experimentation and the de-velopment of complex new techniques and devices. The scrapping of rhetoric, the return to everyday speech, the banning of easy solutions, must be counted among the blessings of a period less interested in the beautiful than in the true, a period in which poetry, if it was to take in the modern scene at all, was obliged, in the phrase of Mr. Eliot's, though applied in another context, "to carry the burdens and exhibit the subtleties of prose".

The cult of sensory reportage, whereby impressions are recorded without their emotional overtones and without any effort to give them a meaning such as synthesis and interpretation might yield, this lack of concern with totality, is partly responsible, no doubt, for the obscurity of a certain kind of contemporary verse. The breakdown of shared systems of reference and the substitution of private ones and even of private semantics, not to mention the taking for granted, in the reader, of an erudition he does not possess— these are further contributory causes of what has humorously been termed "cross-word-puzzle poetry".* It must be admitted that the reading of much of the verse of our time is a task rather than a joy—a labor to be rewarded, perhaps, after long effort and soul-searching, by a sort of delayed enlightenment that, supposedly, more than makes up for all the toil and tedium involved. That this is as it should be, where

* One is comforted with regard to it by remembering a passage from *Alice in Wonderland*: " 'If there's no meaning in it', said the King, 'that saves a world of trouble, you know, as we needn't try to find any.' "

"serious" poetry is concerned, is the position probably taken by a very considerable number of "serious" readers today. This somewhat awe-struck attitude is revealed in the following excerpt from a review by a well-known critic and writer on poetry:* ". . . both the writing and the reading of it involve . . . a kind of exalted drudgery. Its rewards crystallize slowly, like those of a long and painful analysis; sometimes we hardly recognize them as such at all. The solitary effort that a good poem asks, so often without conferring a conscious pleasure . . ." etc.

Here we come upon one of the chief characteristics of the poem in a period even more troubled than most: the absence of the delight normally associated with the experience of poetry. This is not to say that delight represents all that is to be derived from this experience, or that a poem of the first order is going to yield its secrets to any but a qualified reader, willing to bring to it the humility and the surrender that any complex work of art demands. But, whatever else a poem may be, it should be enjoyable. "This must console . . . those who had begun to doubt the wisdom of their own habit of not bothering to read a poet who bored them."**

The truly obscure poem—that is to say, the poem

* Bette Richart, reviewing Edwin Muir's *One Foot in Eden,* in *The Commonweal* of August 3, 1956.
** Anthony Cronin, "A Massacre of Authors", *Encounter,* April 1956.

not easily susceptible of apprehension, much less of comprehension—makes for laborious reading, too often unrewarded. For as enjoyment is one of the avenues that lead to understanding, so understanding is one of the components essential to enjoyment. Mr. Eliot, in his lecture, "The Frontiers of Criticism", delivered on April 30, 1956, at the University of Minnesota—a lecture on the New Criticism, in which the importance of enjoyment as over against mere explication* is emphasized—has summed it up succinctly when he says ". . . I do not think of enjoyment and understanding as distinct activities—one emotional and the other intellectual. . . . It is certain that we do not fully enjoy a poem unless we understand it; and, on the other hand, it is equally true that we do not fully understand a poem unless we enjoy it."

Meaning that escapes analysis—and every true poem is a bit of magic, much of which escapes analysis—is experienced unconsciously through enjoyment. Some of us may not agree with Dryden that

* May not the present dearth of oncoming scientists, technicians and engineers in the United States, be accounted for by the large number of young men who write, for the learnèd quarterlies, essays in which a poem is taken apart like a machine or analyzed as if it were the contents of a test-tube—spiritual descendants, perhaps, of Hudson Maxim, the inventor, who published, in 1910, *The Science of Poetry and Philosophy of Language?*

the chief, if not the only, end of poetry is to delight. All of us will probably agree that the delight it gives us, in the course of giving us other things, is one of its chief virtues. Delight is a means to revelation, and accompanies it.

Our day is a day of judgment. Man has been brought face to face, at last, with "the unpersuadable justice". Of the choices open to him, only one is compatible with survival. He must make that choice or perish. Perhaps that choice will be made, and our growing human solidarity and hope will be reflected in poems into which the element of delight has come back once more. Then the important gains achieved by experimentation will be consolidated throughout an era of "rational conservatism", dissociation of sensibility will give way to a re-association, fission to fusion, the broken music to a greater harmony consonant with the harmony of a new world. The forces that could bring such a world into being are already, however precariously, at work. There are premonitions of it in the literature of the oncoming generation. A return to lyricism, to a lyrical romanticism, is noticeable in the poetry of England, France, Italy and Germany, as well as among the younger American poets. Possibly there is, as Edwin Muir said, "a permanent substance of poetry, a traditional poetic

method . . . which, even after the most violent dis-
turbances, tend to re-establish themselves".

In the meantime, everything waits upon the hour
that shall mark the final, complete realization, translated into practical terms, of the unity of mankind
—the absolute necessity for mutual give-and-take,
yes even for mutual self-sacrifice. In that hour, should
it come, the poem, "exacting the beautiful from the
good" (to use Richard Wilbur's phrase), will play its
part in reconciling our warring selves, in recalling to
men—oh, not in so many words—that they are one.

❧ 6

ON A CERTAIN RESISTANCE

Poetry. I too dislike it: there are things that are important beyond all this fiddle.

MARIANNE MOORE

The imagination that we spurned and crave.

WALLACE STEVENS

❧ The distinction between the function of the scientist and the function of the poet has always been difficult to define and never more so than today when the concepts arrived at by the inspired suppositions of science, and later proved valid by painstaking investigation, rival in beauty and imaginative insight the creations of poetry. The difference in the nature of the two disciplines or modes of knowledge is so obvious to common sense as to make discussion of it seem absurd. To put this very obvious difference into words, however, is another matter.

[59]

The poet, you may say, is concerned with the concrete. In the particular he uncovers the universal. True—yet here his activity parallels that of the scientist, who from specific events deduces his general laws. The poet, you may then counter, has always been aware of the things that lie beyond sense-perception, and is concerned with them. True again—but "in the past fifty years, under the impulse given by Einstein and Rutherford, science has increasingly turned towards phenomena that lie beyond sense-perception".* Well, you reply, somewhat more confidently now perhaps, how about the early stages of poetic composition? Are not "the initial intuition, the period of careful spade-work, of testing and rejection, the state of 'watchful passivity', and the imaginative leap that may come when least expected",** are not these the stages of an experience peculiar to the poet? No—the scientist grappling with his problem is familiar with all of them.

It was Coleridge, wasn't it, who defined beauty as "unity in variety". We have the word of a scientist*** for it that "science is nothing else than the search to discover unity in the wild variety of nature— . . . All

* *The Times Literary Supplement* for April 12, 1957.
** *Ibid.*
*** J. Bronowski, *Science and Human Values* (The Carnegie Lectures delivered at the Massachusetts Institute of Technology), published by Julian Messner, Inc., New York, 1958.

science," he says, "is the search for unity in hidden likenesses. . . . The scientist looks for order in the appearances of nature by exploring such likenesses. For order does not display itself of itself; if it can be said to be there at all, it is not there for the mere looking . . . order must be discovered and, in a deep sense, it must be created. What we see, as we see it, is mere disorder." Might this not be the voice of a poet describing his own quest? Are we, then, obliged to agree with the conclusions of our authority, when he says: "The discoveries of science, the works of art are explorations—more, they are explosions of a hidden likeness. . . . This is the act of creation, in which an original thought is born, and it is the same act in original science and original art. . . . We re-make nature by the act of discovery, in the poem or in the theorem."?

We haven't got very far, it seems, in our effort to define the distinction between the function of the poet and the function of the scientist! Both appear to be bent on the same errand; to arrive at their goals by much the same road; as poet and as scientist, to explore the same universe. Or do they? In the answer to this question we shall find, perhaps, the solution to our problem.

The universe may be conceived as divided into two parts. There is the outer, objective universe of so-called reality, the quantitive, measurable complex of mass-energy in space-time; and there is the equally real inner, subjective universe, the qualitative, undimensional complex of spirit, of feeling, of experience, which is an image of the objective universe as it is reflected in every consciousness. The inner universe is a part of, and is contained within, the outer structural universe, which, so to speak, overarches and is mirrored in it, as the sky, with its stars, is mirrored in a lake. But here the analogy ends. Mirrored in consciousness, in the world of spirit, the objective universe is, as by a creative fusion, transfigured. It becomes other than it was. A qualitative dimension is added. What was matter revolving through space and time becomes a star. Beauty and meaning have been added. In a deeper sense, then, the inner universe includes and completes the outer structure within which, paradoxically, it is contained.

It is this inner, subjective universe that the poet and every other artist explores. The objective structural order is the field in which the scientist conducts his explorations. As a man, he shares with the poet the world of feeling, the world of experience, but in his explorations as a scientist he is obliged to exile himself from that world and to become, for the time being, at least, an inhabitant of the objective universe. He must divest himself of feeling. He must try to get at reality as it is before it is mirrored in consciousness; before the world of the senses and of emotion has transfigured it; before refraction, as it were, has altered perspective. The poem, the work of art, is also a way of knowing, but it is another way and has reference to another world, the inner world of experience, as opposed to the purely objective universe.

There are, of course, peripheral areas in which poetry and science merge—in which the two worlds explored respectively by each are merged. When we step outside the physical sciences we shall find examples of these. Psychology, for instance, is a science which definitely has reference to the inner world of experience. The psychology of Freud, of Jung, of Rank, is, in its basis, a kind of poetry. Here, though the method and the aim are those of science, the world explored is the world to which poetry, and every other art, has reference.

The difference between the two worlds explored, the one by the poet, the other by the scientist, can best be illustrated by examples of the findings reported by each. Let us take a poem by Thomas Hardy, called "Waiting Both":*

* From *Collected Poems,* by Thomas Hardy, copyright, 1925, by The Macmillan Company. Reprinted by courtesy of The Macmillan Company.

> A star looks down at me,
> And says: "Here I and you
> Stand, each in our degree.
> What do you mean to do—
>   Mean to do?"
>
> I say: "For all I know,
> Wait, and let Time go by,
> Till my change come."—"Just so,"
> The star says: "So mean I—
>   So mean I."

Here, in ten brief lines containing only one word of more than a syllable, we are given a glimpse of the universal order. That order is inexorable. As Whitehead has said, "The laws of physics are the decrees of fate".* The introduction, into the poem, of a subjective element, of a human consciousness, as one of the items involved in this inexorable order, and its juxtaposition to an object as vast, as far away and as different as a star, dramatizes the universality of the law. The dialogue between subject and object, between man and star, is admirably adapted to rendering concrete what is abstract, while the reiteration in the last line of each stanza conveys, with its echolalia, a tragic sense of distance, of impersonality,

*Alfred North Whitehead, *Science and the Modern World*, The Macmillan Company, 1925.

of passive, helpless acceptance. Even the inversion of the usual order, in "I and you," which might be thought to have been forced by the rhyme-scheme, seems, in the context, intentional and right. The inversion gives emphasis to each pronoun, where the normal order would have been banal. In this short poem, we do not merely comprehend, we experience vicariously, through the medium of feeling, rhythm, cadence, rhyme, and all the devices of art, a knowledge, a revelation of a truth.

Now let us take the statement of a scientist. Newton's first law of motion reads: "Every body continues in its state of rest, or of uniform motion in a straight line, except so far as it may be compelled by force to change that state." Here the substance of the knowledge or truth experienced in Hardy's poem is conveyed in factual terms and thereby made available to the intellect as a practical working formula. In these terms it *is* not, and for these purposes it *need* not, be experienced; it need only be comprehended. Hardy, in his lyric, and Newton, in his law, are dealing with the same truth. The two examples quoted represent two different disciplines, two different kinds of knowledge, acquired by the exploration of two different aspects of the universe.

It is not necessary to labor the point. Other examples, from the expressions of poets and scientists,

illustrating the distinction between the kind of knowledge that the poet and the kind of knowledge that
the scientist brings over, will occur to all of us:

> . . . thou canst not stir a flower
> Without troubling of a star*

for instance, illustrates, gives us in terms of feeling,
the human sense of two of the basic tenets of science:
the laws of the conservation of matter and of the conservation of energy. Every act, every event, no matter
how trivial, affects the entire cosmos. These tenets
have, since, been incorporated into, and reaffirmed
by, a broader and more basic concept, the potential
equivalence of matter and energy. In this connection,
note how deliberately purified of those elements that
have the qualitative, emotional connotations capable
of arousing in us a sense of vicarious experience is
Einstein's famous expression, $E = mc^2$, deduced in
1905 as one of the first fruits of his amazingly heuris-
tic Relativity Theory. In that expression, an equation
takes the place of language, to announce that meas-
urements of inertia and energy can be calculated from
one another by a simple conversion of the units involved, and to suggest, as has since been abundantly
demonstrated, that what we call matter and energy
are mutually transformable physical states. Matter is

* From "The Mistress of Vision" by Francis Thompson.

[66]

energy, energy is matter—one is inevitably reminded of Keats's "Beauty is truth, truth beauty," an assertion certainly less verifiable and one that has had fewer consequences for the world.

The knowledge of the objective universe that the scientist claims to have brought back with him from his explorations—whether as the result of a hypothesis, or of deduction from known facts, or of a new combination of such facts—can be tested empirically and, if proven valid, becomes a truth until such time as further knowledge calls for further adjustment and modification. What the poet feels he has discovered and made available in the process of his poem must stand the test of another kind of verification. The knowledge he claims to have revealed is a knowledge of the subjective universe of emotion and experience, and the touchstone here is the human spirit inhabiting that universe. To meet the test, to find acceptance as true knowledge, a poem must win the acquiescence in it of another mind. This is no easy matter. Reality so far transcends anything we can say about it as to make silence, for the most part, preferable. Silence says it better. Words too often violate the innocent nobility of things. Where our deepest feelings are concerned, only the spokesman supremely qualified will be tolerated. The statements of science, once checked with observable phenomena and found to embody true knowledge, are accepted as such and soon taken for granted. They are, moreover, as already remarked, subject to constant change as fresh findings make it necessary to amend or revise them. Not so the discoveries of the poet. These reach to the permanent heart of experience. They represent, always, a fresh revelation of an old, perhaps a forgotten, knowledge. We are not, ordinarily, receptive to having such a knowledge revived in us.

There exists in all of us a deep, instinctive, natural resistance to poetry. This resistance may manifest itself in one of several reactions: indifference, embarrassment, ridicule, or acute aversion. Marianne Moore indicates that she sympathizes with the last of these when she says, in her poem entitled "Poetry", "I, too, dislike it: there are things that are important beyond all this fiddle", and Nietzsche, himself a poet in the larger sense of the word, registers that same natural resistance, in the form of combined ridicule and contempt, when he is moved to cry out, "The poets? The poets lie too much". Plato, who declared that poets would be banished altogether from his ideal republic, might, perhaps, have agreed with him. And how many a schoolboy would agree with Plato! How many a grown man or woman has experienced, in the presence of poetry, sensations ranging from a mild embarrassment to an acute distaste!

The kind of knowledge a poem offers us is a renewed awareness, a vicarious re-experience of the
world in all its sensory and emotional impact. This
awareness is lost to us, for the greater part of the time,
in the act of living. In a sense, this lack of awareness may be a safeguard or even an unconscious
self-protection. As Mr. Eliot has told us, "human
kind/ Cannot bear very much reality". Feeling, coiled
in us like the spring of a watch, may find release only
through the gradual, controlled unwinding of the
years. To be conscious, except very occasionally, of
the beauty, sadness, horror and mystery of the human
condition would be more than the human spirit could
endure.

Over our potential responses, our deeply buried
emotions, a normal resistance stands guard. A native
wariness, an instinctive reserve, bulwark us against
the onslaughts of the poet. But these defences are
like the sonic barrier: the poet whose energy and
craft enable him to break through them will meet with
no further obstruction. Renewed awareness, the re-
experience of carefully forgotten reality, that a poem
awakens, is, after all, once it has been achieved for
us, a great good. A heightening and widening of consciousness then takes place, affording insights and
exaltations that do not persist and cannot, perhaps,
even be recalled during the lower, more comfortable,

moments of life. Aldous Huxley wrote, of one of his characters, that he believed in God, but only while the violins were playing, and who is there who hasn't suffered diminishment on leaving the concert hall and finding himself once more in the noisy city street? He has been breathing another air, and is now "rejected into the world again". The point is that, as animals, we are anchored to this world by innumerable necessities, and our mistrust of that other realm of intensified feeling, insight and realization, which, at best, we can inhabit only momentarily, is instinctive and even, perhaps, necessary. It can be overcome by those few only who command the appropriate skills and strategies.

In the making of a poem the creative impulse and the critical faculty must be equally matched. If the impulse is not strong enough and resourceful enough, there will be no poem; if the critical faculty is lacking or not sufficiently active, the poem that may result will be fatuous. Its claim on us as knowledge will be false, it will not tally with experience, it will not be able to disarm our resistance to it. He who would win our suffrage must be self-critical. The normal human reserve, the normal resistance to the kind of knowledge recovered by poetry, the kind of awareness it arouses, will first be encountered, and dealt with, by a true poet, in himself. In him, of all men, that resistance will be strongest. Indeed, his place in the hierarchy might almost be determined by the strength of that resistance and, therefore, the corresponding strength of the impulse and the resourcefulness of the skills required to overcome it—first, in the poet himself, and, later, in others. For by overcoming it in himself, he has, in advance, as it were, overcome it in others also.

The strategies whereby the poet is enabled to outwit our natural resistance to poetry are many and various. They are directed towards arousing us from an inborn, self-protective apathy, towards lulling our active aversion to anything that tries to shock us out of the sleep of habit, the sleep of daily living, into a painful, if exalted, realization of the act of living and of life itself. Our natural, and probably wholesome, apathy is a deep and stubborn thing. This normal, self-protective indifference is not easily overcome. To try to overwhelm us by frontal attack, by putting things down "in so many words," as we say, will not avail. If we are to have our eyes opened to a knowledge, if we are to be forced into renewed experience, we shall have to be tricked and startled out of our apathy. The trope or metaphor, the simplest and commonest strategic device in the arsenal of poetry, does just this. By discovering hidden likenesses or analogies in things, the poem surprises us, wrenches us, if you will, into renewed awareness of them.

All words are, of course, symbols. Many of them,

and particularly compound words, originally were metaphors. But they have become worn with use. Fresh metaphors, compounded of a number of words in new relationships, are needed. The word "white-caps", for instance, denoting the foam scuffed up by wind in its passage over water, has lost, because of familiarity, its original metaphoric force, but when Swinburne describes whitecaps as ". . . where the wind's feet shine along the sea", they are not merely identified, they are experienced once more. Such lines or phrases as "Time is a harper who plays until you fall asleep", "Among the guests star-scattered on the grass", ". . . not even the rain has such small hands", ". . . hung like those top jewels of the night", achieve this immediacy by use of the same device.

Sometimes a metaphor or simile will occur in the midst of, or toward the close of, a poem so casually and unobtrusively as to seem almost accidental and yet will instantly cause everything that has gone before, or that comes after it, to fall into place. The knowledge rediscovered by the poem is, in that instant, by that simile, as blindingly revealed as a familiar landscape by a flash of lightning. This may be observed in a poem by Léonie Adams, "Song from a Country Fair". The poem describes a country dance, attended by the village folk. We hear the fiddles and watch the older couples step out gaily and half-humorously to the music. The young people, whose eagerness and intensity of feeling cause them to hang back in shyness, do not at first participate. Then, in the last two lines, we have the simile that suddenly illuminates all:

> The heart is not so light at first
> But heavy like a bough in spring.

An old knowledge, a familiar but probably forgotten knowledge, that it is those who are most concerned and who care most—in this instance, the young— who can least participate and who will appear to care least, while those who are less involved and who care less—in this instance, the old—can take part more fully and with an apparent easy abandon, this is the knowledge we re-experience in the poem, and the flash of illumination afforded by the simile is what has made that re-experience possible. No amount of exposition or direct statement could so completely have achieved it.

Again, we might include the single miraculously right word in its divinely appointed place. Ezra Pound's "Envoi" to his poem, "Hugh Selwyn Mauberly", concludes with the lines:

> When our two dusts with Waller's shall be laid,
> Siftings on siftings in oblivion,

Till change has broken down
All things save beauty alone.

It is not difficult to put one's finger on the word that here does the work of ten. "Siftings" turns the bare statement of the line above it into full realization. Santayana, in almost the last poem he wrote, "The Poet's Testament", performs a similar miracle. The use of the word "furrow", in the context of the following lines, would mark any writer as a poet:

I give back to the earth what the earth gave,
All to the furrow, nothing to the grave.

An example equally outstanding is Yeats's phrase, ". . . meagre girlhood's putting on/ Burdensome beauty . . ." where the word "burdensome", in one stroke, not only brings the whole picture alive and sums up, for all time, the transition from girlhood to young womanhood, but comments on it as well.

Another device is the use of narrative or drama, complete in itself on one level but employed to symbolize something not explicit that is, nevertheless, on another level, the poem's true concern. The entire poem, then, might be said to be a single complex metaphor. By means of this, the poet is enabled to slip over, unbeknownst as it were, on the wary reader, the knowledge he has re-discovered. If, as Mr. Eliot has written, "the chief use of the meaning of a poem, in the ordinary sense [and here he is careful to state that he is speaking of some kinds of poetry and not all] may be to satisfy one habit of the reader, to keep his mind diverted and quiet, while the poem does its work upon him: much as the imaginary burglar is always provided with a bit of nice meat for the house-dog," then we may compare the device we are now discussing to the ladder that makes it possible for that burglar, if he is a second-story man, to gain entrance to the house while its owner is busy, in his downstairs study, paying the monthly bills.

The poetry of all periods offers notable instances of the use of this device. The dialogue between poet and raven, in Poe's well known poem; the ancient mariner and his account of his voyage, in Coleridge's famous ballad; the Brooklyn Bridge, in Hart Crane's lyrical epic of America: these show us this method at work. The true concern of each of these poems, the knowledge they represent and indirectly bring through, is something other than their surfaces indicate. At the same time that these surfaces are engaging our attention, their underlying power as metaphors, as symbols, is communicating, almost unconsciously, to those capable of receiving it, the actual substance of the poem.

A well known example, of comparatively recent origin, "The Listeners", by Walter de la Mare, illustrates the functioning of this device. The narrative episode that constitutes the symbolism of the poem is as simple as it is subtle and strange. A horseman, who is referred to as "the Traveler", knocks on the moonlit door of a house somewhere in a forest. There is no sound from within and the door is not opened. He knocks again, harder this time, and shouts, "Is there anybody there?" There is no answer, but in the silence that follows, the Traveler senses, in the house, the presence of listeners—their stillness is the only response they make to his question. Suddenly, he knocks on the door a third time, even harder than before, and cries out, "Tell them I came, and no one answered, that I kept my word." Again, there is no reply. No sound, till the silence is interrupted, for a moment, by the beat of plunging hoofs, growing fainter and fainter, as horse and rider gallop away. This, we are given to understand, and every word the Traveler has said, were heard by the listeners in the moonlit house.

> Aye, they heard his foot upon the stirrup,
>   And the sound of iron on stone,
> And how the silence surged softly backward,
>   When the plunging hoofs were gone.

The narrative suspense of the above brief episode, self-sufficient and fully achieved as an account of an action and its dénouement, holds us so completely that the poem, in the meantime, is able to arouse in us a consciousness of the deeper thing it was intended to convey. That thing is a knowledge of, an awareness of, mystery. It is peculiarly fitting, therefore, that what the narrative symbolizes should itself remain a riddle, a mystery. Is the Traveler who knocks on the door a symbol of perplexed humanity, with its stubborn questioning, its probing of the atom and the cell, its knocking on every gate and every door, sensing, behind the façade of appearance, presences, powers there, that could give us the answer if they but would? Does not the cry, before departure, "Tell them I came, and no one answered, that I kept my word", sum up that human quest and its frustration? Or is the confrontation of the Traveler with the listeners the old confrontation of the living with the dead, the bafflement before the inscrutable division that has been made of us into two societies no longer on speaking terms with each other? Many interpretations can be put upon the story that the poem tells, and all of them are somehow merged and blended in the awareness it awakens in us.

A similar use of narrative employed to communicate obliquely the true essence of a poem will be found in Vachel Lindsay's "The Chinese Nightingale". We have here, ostensibly, a story about a

Chinese laundryman, Chang by name, who is discovered, late one night, at work in his laundry. The
background could not well be more drab or the cen-
tral figure more commonplace. As the night wears on,
the barrier between the reality of the workaday world
and the reality of an ancient, now only to be im-
agined, world of the greatest charm and distinction,
falls away. The tiny laundry widens into the king-
dom of pre-Confucian China. The joss in the corner
comes alive, and a small gray bird, a nightingale,
perches on his wrist and begins to sing. The Chinese
princess now appears, who, in some previous incarna-
tion, had been the belovèd of Chang—in those days
a king—and there is dialogue in which the joss, the
nightingale and the princess take part. Chang, the
laundryman, alone is silent, ironing away. The contrast between Chang's former glory, as related by the
princess, and his present fallen state, and between
the image of a long since vanished civilization, and
the tawdry interior of a Chinese laundry on a San
Francisco street, brings into juxtaposition two worlds
and gives one a sense of the equal evanescence of
both. The nightingale serves as chorus to the drama.
So much for the device used. What it actually brings
over, so subtly and insinuatingly as to take the reader
quite off his guard, is the poem's essence. By use of
this device the poet reawakens in us, while we are

absorbed in the drama and the story, an old knowledge: the perpetual recurrence of feeling, of love and
sorrow, of glory and heartbreak; the persistent con-
tinuation of life, for better, for worse, amid the tragic
flux.

> "One thing I remember:
> Spring came on forever,
> Spring came on forever,"
> Said the Chinese nightingale.

All these are ways of suggesting things without saying them in so many words—examples of the strategy
of the oblique approach, whereby the poet surprises
us into attention, beguiles us out of our natural
apathy, circumvents our active resistance to poetry.
As this resistance differs between individual and individual, so it differs between race and race. There has
been less resistance to poetry among the Latins than
among the Anglo-Saxons, among certain Eastern
peoples than among those of the West. The character
of this resistance, too, varies, from period to period.
Every age reveals the resistances peculiar to it, but
all of them are, fundamentally, symptoms of the same
thing, different expressions of the one deep underlying resistance.

The particular elements or qualities in a poem that
have aroused, in the mind of our time, this natural

resistance to poetry might be listed as: emotion directly expressed and the romantic in general; the explicitly personal note; elevation of tone or style; effects whose purpose is aural delight—as, richness of verbal texture, intricacy of form, incantatory magic; and what, for lack of a better term, might be called synthesis, the subduing of parts to a whole. Resistance to emotion directly expressed, and to the romantic, is often circumvented by wit and by devices of tone: irony, indifference, self-mockery, toughness, and so on. Personal themes and lyricism in the first person singular are usually avoided. The language employed is the language of every-day speech, colloquial, even conversational. Resistance to the element of aural delight makes itself felt in the use of dissonance, bare statement, deliberately awkward run-overs, deliberately imperfect form and flawed meter, flat cadence, false rhyme, etc. The poem is likely to confine itself to accurate minute observation of particulars without the coördination that would give the whole thing a meaning beyond that of any of its parts.

These generalizations, like most generalizations, state the case very loosely and clumsily. The instant they are made, exceptions leap to mind: the sonorous incantations of Dylan Thomas, a poet whose work, by its very nature, does not answer to any of the descriptions just given; Wallace Stevens's "Sunday Morning", with its Renoiresque setting and richly colorful verbal texture; the aural beauty of Eliot's austere cadences and haunting repetitions and returns, in such poems as "Ash Wednesday" and "Four Quartets". This poet, in whom the resistances characteristic of the period must have been very strong, was able, by virtue of a poetic impulse still stronger, to devise a poetry that outwitted these resistances and thus fulfilled the requirements of thousands of readers in whom, since they were his contemporaries, the same resistances were to be found.

Mr. Eliot introduced into English poetry a new way of doing things and, from the first, his manner has remained substantially the same. Yeats, on the other hand, offers us the example of a poet whose work, begun in an earlier period and expressive of that period but carried on through a time of transition and into our own day, responded to the changes that came about in the nature of our resistances to poetry as rapidly as these changes, often unconsciously, took place in himself. The poet of the Celtic twilight, the poet of the early romantic, rhetorical poems of love and of Celtic mythology, is barely recognizable in the robust, sometimes savage, realist of the superb later work, the author of such poems as "In Memory of Major Robert Gregory" and "Sailing to Byzantium".*

* From the *Collected Poems* of William Butler Yeats, copyright, 1903, 1904, 1906, 1907, 1908, 1912, 1916, 1918, 1919, 1924, 1925, 1928 and 1933, by The Macmillan Company. Reprinted by courtesy of The Macmillan Company.

WHAT IS POETRY?

The latter may serve to illustrate some of the strategies used by a great poet in dealing with certain contemporary resistances.

The symbolism of "Sailing to Byzantium" is defined in the title—a voyage of escape from the temporal world, the world of nature, to the eternal world of art and of the intellect. This symbolism, and the ritualistic formality and ceremony of the poem's organization, are ingenious devices for circumventing our natural resistance to the unabashed revelation that is the poem's truth: an old man's rage and dismay at the process of physical deterioration; the longing of age, and specifically of the aging artist, to escape from a temporal, disintegrating form into an eternal, unchanging one—into an art form, as Beethoven could be said to have escaped from his body into the symphonies.

Note the conversational tone of the opening lines of the first stanza, with its deliberately colloquial, slightly awkward, first line:

> That is no country for old men. The young
> In one another's arms, birds in the trees,
> —Those dying generations—at their song,
> The salmon-falls, the mackerel-crowded seas,
> Fish, flesh, or fowl, commend all summer long
> Whatever is begotten, born, and dies.
> Caught in that sensual music, all neglect
> Monuments of unageing intellect.

The last two lines, whose studied formality verges on the grandiloquent, have, in the context, an intentionally humorous effect. But here emotion wears, for the most part, the mask of indifference.

In the second stanza, that mask is laid aside, and, in the first four lines, strong feeling, in order to elude our resistance to it, comes over in the guise of a kind of grotesque, self-deprecating mockery. It is as if the poet said, "Look, I'm not being sorry for myself. It's all rather absurd and amusing, really." The effect is twofold: strong feeling is enabled to come through, in disguise; and is heightened, because of the gallantry implicit in the character of the disguise adopted. The tone again, in the first four lines at least, is conversational:

> An agèd man is but a paltry thing,
> A tattered coat upon a stick, unless
> Soul clap its hands and sing, and louder sing
> For every tatter in its mortal dress,
> Nor is there singing school but studying
> Monuments of its own magnificence;
> And therefore I have sailed the seas and come
> To the holy city of Byzantium.

The last four lines of the stanza are, of course, a simple statement of fact, taking up again, and carrying forward, the narrative symbolism of the poem.

In the third stanza, after the restrained appeal of the first four lines, feeling threatens to get out of hand, but manages to by-pass our defences by ex-pressing itself, in the sixth line, in the harshest, coarsest, least romantic terms possible:

> O sages standing in God's holy fire
> As in the gold mosaic of a wall,
> Come from the holy fire, perne in a gyre,
> And be the singing-masters of my soul.
> Consume my heart away; sick with desire
> And fastened to a dying animal
> It knows not what it is; and gather me
> Into the artifice of eternity.

The phrase that refers to the self in old age as "fast-ened to a dying animal" is, to modern sensibility, one of the great moments in the poem. Its harshness, its brutality, like a slap in the face, takes us off our guard, thus permitting direct, personal emotion to assert itself without arousing the resistance to it so strong in contemporary readers. This phrase, "fast-ened to a dying animal", would not have been accept-able in Shelley's time, or in Tennyson's, or even in Swinburne's, when resistance to other elements in poetry—specifically to the unromantic, the "unpoetic" —was equally strong. It would have found ready acceptance in the time of Donne or Swift. The last part of the concluding sentence, "and gather me/ Into the artifice of eternity", reiterates the emotion so violently conveyed before, but, this time, in a state-ment as cold as ice.

In the final stanza, where the symbolism of the poem is further extended and elaborated, the emotion that is the poem's truth is again disguised and, again, is given greater force by that disguise. The mechanical, not to say metallic, character of the metaphor employed to distinguish the world of art from the world of nature contrasts poignantly with the suppressed feeling it embodies. Here emotion wears once more a ceremonial mask:

> Once out of nature I shall never take
> My bodily form from any natural thing,
> But such a form as Grecian goldsmiths make
> Of hammered gold and gold enamelling
> To keep a drowsy Emperor awake;
> Or set upon a golden bough to sing
> To lords and ladies of Byzantium
> Of what is passed, or passing, or to come.

In this magnificent poem, most of the resistances to poetry encountered in contemporary sensibility are faced and dealt with by the strategies of a poet whose poetic character was formed during a period when resistances to quite other elements in poetry prevailed. Emotion here outwits resistance to it by the use of disguise and the device of an intricate symbolism; the directly personal note is ritualized; profound awarenesses are evoked in a poem that employs, for the most part, the language of everyday speech.

[85]

The contemporary resistances to aural delight and to what we have called synthesis are alone ignored.

There have been occasions when the knowledge brought over by science has clashed with the dogmas of the church. At times, this threat has met with the sternest disapproval and opposition. And, entirely apart from its menace to doctrine, such a theory as that of Copernicus, for instance, must have seemed, to the vanity of men, far less flattering than the earlier Ptolemaic theory of the universe had been. Ordinarily, however, the statements of science do not arouse in us the kind of natural resistance we have to the revelations of poetry. Clearly, whatever their practical implications, these statements do not concern us so deeply. They are peripheral and impersonal, they do not touch that inner self that sits at the center of the web of experience.

The statements of science are hearsay, reports from a world outside the world we know. What the poet tells us has long been known to us all, and forgotten. His knowledge is of our world, the world we are both doomed and privileged to live in, and it is a knowledge of ourselves, of the human condition, the human predicament. The measure of our resistance to what the poet would remind us of is the measure of the intensity of our feelings with regard to it. There is, in all of us, a profound longing for the release of these deeply suppressed, inarticulate feelings. For that very reason, perhaps, where they are involved we find ourselves on the defensive. It is not everyone who is permitted to re-awaken in us these fiercely guarded awarenesses. But for him who, because of his skills, the labors he has undergone, the self-discipline he has endured, is equipped to pierce those defenses, to reach us and give us, despite ourselves, the release we long for—that moment of realization and reconcilement beyond the chaos of things —for him we have reserved a name that has blessèd associations, the name of poet.

7

THE PROCESS AND THE POEM

It begins in delight and ends in wisdom.

FROST

  "Since you give yourselves out to be poets, let's see you command poetry" ("Gebt ihr euch einmal für Poeten/ So commandiert die Poesie"), this injunction, addressed by the director of the theatre to the theatre's poet, in the Prologue to Goethe's *Faust*, sums up the first and instinctive reaction of the many who do not understand why a poet, if he has anything to say, can't sit down and write it out in plain language, without more ado or fuss about it. Later, however, learning that the matter is far more complicated and esoteric than this, most of these good people rush to the other extreme and succumb to one of the oldest and most widely held of notions regarding poetic composition. Socrates him-

[88]

self must have succumbed to it, for he said, "The utmost that mere art can produce is as nothing compared to what can be produced in the state of mania." According to this theory, a poet finds the words for what he wants to say in moments of almost supernatural excitation and clairvoyance known as "inspiration", during which state lines and stanzas, or even the whole poem, may take form in his mind with little or no conscious effort. Such things have, of course, happened—there is the famous example of Coleridge's "Kubla Khan"—but they are the exception rather than the rule, and for a very good reason, as we shall see. Poets themselves have been largely responsible for the currency of this myth, not out of dishonesty but out of the self-deception incident to the excitement of creation. The creation of a new thing, when by a happy combination of skill, labor, and good fortune this has been permitted to come to pass, partakes of the miraculous. To the maker, in the triumph and elation of achieved realization, it does not seem that he could have accomplished it of himself, unaided. From the very first, faced with an almost insuperable task, he had felt his own inadequacy. Has not the poet, from the beginning of time, called upon the Muse to enable him to do the impossible! So that when, after long torment and frustration, what had appeared impossible has been achieved, you cannot blame him if he persuades himself, as Blake did, that he has written "from immediate dictation . . . without premeditation, and even against my will."

Why may we feel certain that neither of the above notions regarding poetic composition has or could have general validity? Why shouldn't a poet sit down and write out, in plain language, whatever it is he wants to say? On the other hand, why may it not be that, knowing what he wants to say but not how to say it, the unconscious part of him—some outside agency, if you prefer—takes over and says it for him and far better than he ever could? Both questions show a misunderstanding of the poetic process as testified to by the experience of poets, and both can be answered as follows: "Because a poet first learns what it is that he wants to say by trying to say it; the gradual working out of the poem itself is what gives eventual definition to the more or less undefined impulse that prompted it." The reference here is, obviously, to the pure poem, the lyric poem, and not to the narrative, dramatic, or occasional poem, where subject is predetermined.

From the unbroken continuity and flow of things, the chaos of appearances, the mind isolates certain aspects and then assembles them into separate images and patterns of meaning. These represent the first

and most direct form of knowledge. The colors, out-
lines, and dimensions of one part of a continuous
landscape, for instance, will become, when mind has
thus isolated and assembled them, a tree. So automatic
and habitual is this function of mind that we are
unaware of it. Indeed, after early childhood, it is
probably impossible for us, when looking at a tree,
to experience uncombined into one particular pattern
of meaning the various sensuous components from
which we have constructed it—to see it, in other
words, in any other way than as a tree.

But there can be occasions when we catch in the
act, so to speak, this process in which mind is con-
tinuously and automatically engaged. Lying late in
bed perhaps, on a Sunday morning, in the delicious
state between waking and sleeping that precedes full
consciousness, you find yourself examining an unfamiliar animal that seems to have curled itself up on
the sofa at the other end of the room. The color and
contours of this creature suggest a smallish brown
dog; the head appears to be down and turned away, so
as to be only partly visible, and the whole position,
including the curve of the back, indicates sleep. In
fact, on more intense scrutiny, a faint, regular, very
slow movement of the body, rising and falling rhyth-
mically, is clearly perceptible. It's very puzzling. How
does he come to be there? Without bothering to get

up, you study him more closely. And then—presto, it's done! Mind, in a flash, has re-assembled color, contour, and other visual data into the brown blanket you brought in before going to bed and left lying on the sofa. From that instant on, no amount of imaginative effort will enable you to reconstruct out of that crumpled blanket the dog you saw there only a moment ago. You can now see it as a blanket only. A blanket it is and a blanket it remains.

Just as certain sense impressions, selected out of the welter of appearances, are thus assembled by mind into images and patterns of meaning, the simplest form of knowledge, with the result that one such combination of colors, contours, dimensions, and so forth, becomes what we call a tree, another a horse, still another a mountain, so these same images and patterns, as well as the more intricate complexes of experience, have the potentiality, when themselves assembled and combined in a work of art, of yielding larger patterns, a profounder form of knowledge. The feeling out of which a poem grows may be described as the awareness, on the part of a poet, of such a potentiality latent in a given combination. At this point, he knows nothing more than that he is on the verge of some meaningful discovery. For the moment, he is seeing, as we say—that is, experiencing—familiar things in a strangely unfamiliar way. These images, patterns of meaning, complexes of experience, in whose presence, as it were, he stands, and in whose combination, if he can find the clue, he senses the possibility of a synthesis that shall be a new entity, namely the poem, have suddenly become transfigured, are charged with some as yet indefinable significance. They have taken on a new character, a new urgency, a new insistence. Such the wild swans at Coole must have taken on for Yeats, when their presence there, in combination with the physical background and its associations and his own mood, stirred in him the first glimmerings of a knowledge that became articulate in the poem of that title and was gradually defined for him in the process of making it. Such the daffodils, for Wordsworth. Such the sea and the cemetery, in their juxtaposition, for Valéry, when the combination sent him groping toward the secret ultimately so completely surrendered to the sonorous achievement of his "Le Cimetière Marin".

It is at this moment of his greatest excitement, at the moment when he senses that some mystery is about to be divulged to him, that a poet must learn to observe the strictest circumspection. As a landscape painter may put his head between his legs to get a fresh point of view or a portrait painter watch the sitter out of the corner of his eye while directing his gaze elsewhere, a poet at this juncture will avoid concentrating the focus of his mind too intently on the yet undefined significance with which the objects of his contemplation have so mysteriously become endowed. He is in the position of a man who woos a disdainful and capricious woman. An assumed nonchalance and indifference, a studied turning of the attention elsewhere, are essential at this point. Too steady a concentration on the mysterious significance with which the objects of contemplation seem, for the moment, to have become endowed, too avid a greed to wrest the final secret from them, can have only one result: their special significance will ebb from these objects—the wild swans at Coole will be seen again as the quite usual, very beautiful birds they are; the daffodils will become yellow flowers; the sea and the cemetery will be a sea and a cemetery— and the secret so ruthlessly grappled for will be lost. In other words, if you look at anything too steadily, you will no longer see it; if you pursue the quarry too openly, you will frighten it away.

The truth that is a poem must, like any wild thing, be stalked; it will never be taken alive by direct assault. Step by step, and with assumed unconcern, the poet approaches. Stealthily, through endless circles of trial and error, revision and elimination, he saunters around the prey. Line by line and sentence by sentence, its form and contours grow clearer. The net of language is flung; coil by coil, loop by loop, it is tightened until, at long last, coming up with his catch, the poet is able to examine and to understand what it is he has, so long, so arduously, and so deviously, been pursuing. The thing he may find there will often astound him.

The worst that can happen to a poem in the making is to have its truth, its secret, stated in premature form and therefore only half-stated. The knowledge potential in it has then been imperfectly crystalized. Once so fixed in the rigidity of words, it is difficult to dissolve it back into its elements, for re-formation. This is what will occur when any of the stages in the gradual process of clarification are evaded by reason of haste and over-eagerness. The final freezing into language must be postponed until every possibility has been explored while the poem is still in its fluid state. The ultimate choice, the ultimate decision, implies the elimination of all the possibilities not chosen. The truth of the poem, which, because of these, was as boundless as it was vague, must now shrink into its sharp and single definition representing among all possibilities, if the choice has been wisely made, the survival of the fittest. Yet, however wisely this choice has been made, the finished poem, because of this shrinkage, will seem to the poet something less than the initial feeling of it had promised. For this reason also, he should be reluctant to make the final commitment.

The poet, from the beginning of time, has been a target for ridicule as much as he has been an object of veneration. Rhyme, especially, for those who do not understand its nature and its function—and it can be one of the most effective elements in a poem—has always run the risk of appearing to be a mere convention, as absurd as it is artificial. This view has been shared by poets themselves—one has only to think of Milton, Whitman, the Imagists, and others. Even Gautier, distinguished for his expert and delicious use of rhyme, pokes fun at those poets who, as he says, spend their days dealing with the end-words of lines and, having successfully matched *âme* and *flamme, ombre* and *sombre, dieu* and *lieu,* cross their legs, fold their arms, and sit back in smug satisfaction, permitting the stars in heaven to resume once more their accustomed orbits.

Perhaps the commonest among the slightly ludicrous popular conceptions of the poet is that of one with his head in the clouds, an overly emotional man, constantly swept off his feet in a surge of excitement by things that the average man accepts without undue elation or perturbation. While it is true that the poet enjoys a greater immunity from the numbing and anaesthetizing effect that the act of living, with all its routines and repetitions, produces in most of us, so that he is the man, above all others, who takes experience the least for granted, the man in whom the sense of wonder and delight is still as alive as it is with the run of men only in childhood, he must nevertheless when at work be as cold, as level-headed, and as detached as a surgeon. To understand what is only dimly felt, what is only gradually taking form, and to understand it well enough to be able to render it objective, even to oneself, in words, requires the virtues of a severely analytic mind. Further, to take what is conceived in the excitement of the imagination and so to articulate it in language that it will not only meet the test of scrutiny, by sober daylight, of another mind but have the power to break through the defenses of that mind and rouse it from the sleep of habit, and a normal apathy, to renewed awareness, this calls for supreme self-command, for the cold, deliberate precision of art. A poet must be both more and less impassioned than other men. His prayer as artist could not be summed up better than in Eliot's words: "Teach us to care and not to care./ Teach us to sit still."

At this point it might be said, "So far, so good, but how about the end-product, the poem itself? We are less interested in the process of poetic composition than we are in the results and in what gives one poem greater significance or seriousness than another. Is there any criterion in respect to this?" The answer might be that if we consider a poet as engaged in exploring the inner world, the world of experience, and a poem as the knowledge he brings back with him from his exploration, then the significance or seriousness of a poem will depend upon the extent of the area explored and the depth to which that exploration has been effective. Subject matter will have little to do with it, or mere brilliance of execution. A poem about God may be less "serious" than a poem about a goldfish, a *tour de force* of technical virtuosity than a poem less accomplished, a humorous or satiric poem may deserve the adjective more than does the gravest metaphysical discourse. Nor is relevance to its particular period necessarily a qualification, for what was relevant to one period may prove to have relevance to no other. The final arbiter will not be the audience in space, the mass audience at any given moment, but the audience in time, the qualified reader throughout the ages.

Men are divided by many things other than war. A great poem, despite the barriers of language, unites men as does any great work of art. A work of art represents a remission, a truce, in the midst of the endless struggle in which all are engaged. In its presence, the participants and opponents in that struggle come together no longer as such but as disinterested spectators of the whole tragi-comic drama and predicament of life. It is not so much that, at these times, we become united, as that our essential unity, lost sight of in the stress of the struggle, is then brought home to us anew. For a moment we are seeing more clearly, having a larger vision, from a vantage point above the arena of conflict. The mask falls from the face of the enemy and reveals a fellow creature, victim, like ourselves, of the tragic nature of things.

≈§ 8

SOME THOUGHTS ON POETRY

> *One hardly ever sees any more a product of the desire for perfection. . . . Novelty, intensity, strangeness—in a word, all the values of surprise —have supplanted it.*
>
> VALÉRY

≈§ It is doubtful whether consciousness, a phenomenon originated and developed in the interests of survival, and sustained from moment to moment only by the most delicate balance, the most gigantic labor—the organs of the body functioning in perfect coördination, the heart hurling its oxygen-bearing blood-stream through the brain at the rate of seven and a half pounds a second—it is doubtful whether this inestimable treasure, purchased at so great a cost, is fully appreciated by any of us. The deeply rooted fear of death, the passion for continuance, a passion heightened perhaps by the suspicion that life is a

SOME THOUGHTS ON POETRY

gift vouchsafed but once, or, as Rilke has it, ". . . Einmal/ jedes, nur einmal. Einmal und nicht mehr. . . ." (. . . Once/ to each, once only. Once and no more. . . .)—these bear witness, on the instinctual level, to the value we attach to consciousness. But we are speaking now of the rarer, the more articulate appreciation of this surpassing thing, so often taken for granted, that affords us, as it were, a window on the huge spectacle of being; the antennae by which we receive vibrations from the outer world, the touch of a hand, the light of a star; that exquisite mirror where, as in still water, the trembling of the tiniest leaf, and the slow drift of the clouds across heaven, are reflected, the whole magical kaleidoscopic panorama of things out of whose forms and patterns we weave the individual fantasy that is our life, and whose pleasures, joys, yes and ecstasies, so greatly exceed—though there are hours when we forget this —all the toils, pains and agonies we pay for the privilege of consciousness. Death itself, so inexorably and inevitably exacted in the end, will be, we are forced to admit, not too high a price to pay for that privilege, the privilege of having lived, of having experienced consciousness, even if once only.

The world reflected in consciousness is a world in perpetual flux; consciousness is itself in flux. Our shifting moods, the result of impulses from within

and reactions to forces from without, may be likened
to the interplay of light and shade in a countryside
under wind-driven clouds, or to the restless flow of
music, rising, turning, falling, deepening, rising
again, then saddening, fading, brightening, unfold-
ing into new and endless patterns and progressions.
Amid these never-ceasing passages of consciousness
there will occur moments, or combinations of moments, that seem to be endowed with a mysterious
significance, a singular perfection. Is the impulse
at the root of art the impulse that prompted Goethe's
Faust to cry out, in the presence of such a moment,
"Verweile doch, du bist so schön!" (O stay awhile,
thou art so beautiful!)? Is the poem an artifact for
recording and preserving such a moment, rescuing it
from the flux of time, placing it above and beyond
time in a form where it may offer forever, to all who
seek it out, a renewal of the experience that made it
so memorable? If we are to credit the testimony of
poets with regard to the making of a poem or are
capable of analyzing the source of our own pleasure
in the reading of it, we shall be led to the conclusion
that the impulse out of which a poem grows is not
so much the desire to salvage a bit of experience
from the flux in which all experience is involved as
it is the need to render objective, and so to understand, the intimations of some order, some pattern of

meaning, that seem to emanate from certain combinations amid the general chaos. Art seeks a knowledge, gradually defined in its very process. Delight is a means toward the achievement of that knowledge, and the achievement itself results in delight—the recognition of something we have dimly sensed, or known and forgotten, now re-discovered, now first fully revealed.

Popular misconceptions notwithstanding, the medium in which poetry operates is more refractory than that of any of the other arts. Almost all of us read and write, we make daily use of language, and are inclined to underestimate its difficulties and the problems it poses for a poet. The very fact that the medium of our most casual intercourse, our everyday commonplaces, is also the medium of our highest form of expression, of poetry itself, constitutes one of the handicaps under which the art labors. As if it were not enough that language fluctuates with usage and is constantly changing, that words alter in value, shedding old denotations and connotations and taking on new auras of tone and implication, there is the damage done to them by wear and tear. The bloom rubs off words that are wrongly employed, or too often employed to trivial purposes. Words can go numb with the familiarity that comes from over-use, or, indeed, with the familiarity that comes from too long a contemplation of them, as every poet, sooner or later, discovers. He will have to put the difficult poem, with its problems, aside and return to it only when the feeling and tone of the words shall have been revived for him.

None of the other arts suffers to the same degree as does poetry from this handicap of a medium too often charged with trivial associations—music, perhaps, the least of all. Moreover, like music, poetry suffers from the limitations shared by the arts that function in time. The instant unity of effect in a work every part of which can be comprehended simultaneously is possible only to the plastic or visual arts. Though the amount of detail visible to the eye decreases with distance, the extent of the area that can be taken in at a glance is proportionately increased. It is a curious fact that the experience of simultaneity is denied to every sense except those of sight and touch. Two odors, two flavors, may not be experienced simultaneously: merging, they form a compound odor, or flavor, quite distinct in character from either component. In the same way, three separate notes, sounding simultaneously, will lose their individual identity and become a chord. Even this modified simultaneity, which music attains through harmony and the blending of orchestral voices, where each instrument, nevertheless, sounds different notes, is not permitted to poetry. Two voices reading different poems simultaneously will not complement but drown each other out. Wasn't it the Dada-ists who delighted in having a poet read aloud from his work while another, on the same platform, rubbed two pieces of sandpaper together so effectively as to make it impossible for the first to be heard?

The painter, the sculptor, has but to step back a few paces in order to appraise, at a glance, the proportions and over-all design of the work in progress. How much more difficult is this for the composer, the novelist, the poet, unable at any given moment to stand off and survey his creation as a whole! Few minds are capable of keeping in view, throughout every part of a work, over long periods of time and under varying moods and circumstances, the vision of the grand scheme, the total design, so clearly and steadily as to give all parts their proper inter-relationships, their due proportionate weight and emphasis within the general structure that they compose but whose unity transcends them. What labors will the requirements of an art functioning in time often imply! It is told of Pushkin that while at work on *Eugene Onegin* he was in the habit of going over, each morning, all he had previously written of this novel in verse, so as to re-establish in his mind, before building further, the shape and pattern of the whole thing to date.

If you add, to the difficulties for which the relativity and instability of language are responsible, the difficulties encountered by an artist whose medium is temporal rather than spatial, you will get some notion of the torments of the poet. Lessing, in his *Laokoön*, has analysed for us the distinctive capabilities and limitations of the respective arts. Sometimes, however, you will come across examples that seem to prove that his assignment of the narrative as the domain of poetry, and of the descriptive as the domain of painting, is true exactly in reverse. With what immediacy, for instance, does the proportioned solidity of the forms in Michelangelo's painting, "The Temptation of Adam and Eve", bring home to us the story of which the action depicted is but the crucial moment! The woman-snake, coiled around trunk and bough of the Tree of Knowledge, is shown offering the forbidden apple to Eve, while Adam assists by pulling down the branch. The three figures, Adam, Eve, and the snake, compose one unified pattern of movement. All parts of the picture, including the overshadowing tree that serves as background, are simultaneously experienced. What is thus conveyed, in an instant of time, apart from the marvelous plasticity of the forms, is drama, is narrative. Milton, in his "Paradise Lost", requires many pages of verse to record the action here reaching its climax, and the dramatic impact of the great moment itself is impaired by the elaborate preparatory exposition. In the poem, as if to disprove Lessing's thesis, what holds the imagination is not the narrative element but the descriptive charm, the subtlety of pictorial evocation. Painting and poem alike are charged with the all-pervasive sense of form that distinguishes the work of these two masters of the grand style. Form, like a gravitational field, permeates every portion of an achieved creation and, like gravity, operates to bind all parts together around one common center. The artist may feel that the necessities and requirements of form are restrictive, are weighing him down, that he is contending against them, and rising above them, at moments, by the exercise of sheer energy and skill. He forgets that the machine that has enabled man to fly is airborne by virtue of a combination of forward-driving energy and the downward pull of the very gravity against which it contends. An equilibrium has been reached. Form, like gravity, is what makes flight possible.

Form, and the concept of form, have undergone greater and more revolutionary changes during the past fifty years than in any other period of like duration. This has been true of poetry as of the other arts and especially has it been true of American poetry. In the United States, nearly all the younger poets of the past four decades have been teachers by voca-

tion, so that we have had over here what, at almost
any other time, would have seemed an anomaly, not
to say a contradiction in terms—namely, an academic
avant-garde.* Certainly, the great majority of contemporary American poets are learnèd men and
women, holders of Ph.D. degrees, professors of English literature and composition at universities and
colleges. For the first time in our history the practis-
ing poet, with few exceptions, is an individual pro-
fessionally trained in literature, its history and
techniques. In contradistinction to poets like Burns,
Blake, Keats, Rossetti, Whitman and Yeats, who never
went to college, or others like Browning, Coleridge,
Shelley, Swinburne and Tennyson, who attended
but did not graduate, the poet of today is usually
a scholar.** It is natural that, as such, he should take
a rather special interest in the scholarly aspects of
poetry, in the intricacies of allusion and of textual
explication in general, and in the literary techniques
he teaches. The contemporary emphasis, both in
poetry and in criticism, is inevitably on those elements that lend themselves to scholarly interpreta-

* I am indebted, for this phrase, to Geoffrey Grigson; see his
essay, "Mood of the Month IX", in the April 1959 issue of
The London Magazine.
** See "The Present State of Poetry", by Delmore Schwartz, in
American Poetry at Mid-Century, 1958, Superintendent of
Documents, Washington, D.C.

tion and on the work of poets rich in those elements.

The poetry of our time has greatly benefitted by this more wide-spread erudition on the part of poets and of the men and women who have been their pupils. It is undeniable, also, that the scholastic or learnèd side of poetry has attracted to it some individuals whose training and natural endowments equip them to be scientists, technicians, and logicians rather than poets or critics of poetry. One result of this has been a certain amount of writing in verse, and about verse, predicated on the notion that poetry, like mechanics, is an exact science, or that poems exist not to be enjoyed but to be studied, analyzed, and evaluated on the basis of their allusions, underlying system of reference, and arcane mythic and symbolic content, much after the fashion of the psychoanalytic interpretation of dreams. Young couples, vacationing at the seashore, and with little feeling for literature per se but a great deal of spare time on their hands, will devote that spare time to detective work, unravelling the allusions, references and supposed symbolizations of poems or novels they are incapable of enjoying, and therefore will never truly understand, but into which they read elaborate meanings and intentions that would surprise no one more than the author himself. Those, of this mental make-up, who write verse are preoccupied in manufacturing a product that shall, in turn, afford readers and critics similar opportunities for the same sort of literary dissection. And all this, of course, has nothing to do with poetry, and can often be vexatious and annoying.

Most of the poets who are professors, the academic poets of our day, have stood for the exact reverse of the narrow traditionalism and conservatism usually associated with that adjective. Our age has been enriched by the experimentation in which these poets, as well as their fellow painters and composers, have engaged. Indeed, singularity rather than perfection seems to have been, during the last fifty years, the aim of all the arts. Valéry, you will remember, claims that this trend began with the advent of the romantic movement that followed the disintegration of orthodoxy, and of old standards of belief and taste, toward the close of the eighteenth century. "Novelty, intensity, strangeness" have, for us, in our "insatiable thirst for originality", to use his own words, supplanted the ideal of beauty. To be different at all costs has become almost the chief concern. To be called "a rebel", to be characterized as "intrepid", "a dauntless innovator", "a daring modernist", represents, for an artist today, the most signal accolade his peers can bestow upon him. Yet the very word "modern",* fetish of youth and of the advertising profession, is, after all, relative—has no absolute significance. You might think nothing had been modern until we came along. Why, bless us, everything has been modern for the past five thousand years; everything in its day is modern! The title, *An Anthology of Modern Poetry,*** given to a collection issued in 1963, will read strangely to those coming across the book a hundred or even fifty years hence.

Personality or individuality*** is, clearly, the source of originality. Goethe knew this when he wrote, "Sei es Jesu, sei es Buddha,/ Alles ist Persönlichkeit." (Be it Jesus, be it Buddha,/ personality is all.) Our consciousness is not a static thing; rather, it resembles the sliding of brook water over stones. Its flow, like that of brook water, is always forward, and anything that threatens to block that flow—indecision, conflict, too steady and intense a concen-

* Perhaps it is our worship of science that has given this word its halo. In science, what is new, what is modern, will usually mark an improvement. In the arts, this does not necessarily follow.
** Ours is an age of anthologies. What little familiarity with poetry, readers of today enjoy is based very largely upon these collections. No field is immune to the anthology, no title too absurd for it, e.g., *An Anthology of Poems by Women.* (Why not *An Anthology of Poems by Men, A Little Collection of Poems on Drowsiness!*)
*** Coleridge defines personality as "individuality existing in itself, but with a nature as a ground".

tration—is dangerous and will be resisted. The forward process must not be interrupted too long. The way in which it circumvents these obstructions determines the shape of the stream, and this more or less stable shape of the stream of consciousness is what we call personality. The personality represents a compromise between what the original endowment (for our main characteristics reveal themselves very early) has been able to project from within and what environment, circumstance, the necessity of things, has forced upon us from without. There are, in every personality, a nearly infinite number of forms and directions that its development might take, potentialities so diverse as to offer opportunities for the evolution of a great variety of selves. Of these, however, comparatively few can be permitted to come into full being. "The criticism of time," to quote Valéry once more, will delete most of them. Survival itself depends upon the elimination of all except those few that form a manageable combination. The resultant personality represents such a combination of permissible selves, and the stronger, the more unique, the original endowment, the richer and more meaningful will that combination be, representing, as it does, the prevalence of personality, to a greater extent than is usual, over the restrictions imposed upon it from without. Personality is the decisive factor, qua originality, in any work of art, since it determines which, out of the many possibilities clamoring for realization there, shall be selected to survive. As in life itself, the alternative chosen must prove compatible with the ruling necessity—in the case of a work of art, the over-all form.

What one looks for first, then, in a poet, is personality and, after that, good workmanship. Neither, without the other, amounts to much. Their combination will be talent. Personality, as we have seen, implies originality. True originality is unconscious. You cannot be original by an act of will. In every period there are always too many poets trying to be original in exactly the same way. Mere oddities of form or of manner, mere typographical innovations, though they may accompany, do not, of themselves, constitute originality. Originality may reveal itself in work that is traditional just as truly as in work that is experimental. Yeats has as much personality as Whitman, and his work is quite as original. Bach, who brought to its highest perfection the art of music as he found it in his own time, is as original as Beethoven, who gave the development of the symphony a new direction. Good workmanship implies a natural, inborn aptitude and a long self-critical discipline in an art; for poetry, as Mr. Pound has been at pains to remind us, is an art. Good workmanship, without personality—that is to say, without originality—is mere virtuosity, empty technique. Personality, without good workmanship—that is to say, without art—becomes mere eccentricity. Good workmanship doesn't mean solely a disciplined, accomplished skill in the use of language, cadence, rhythm, rhyme, and formal structure. It means this, but it means also a practiced resourcefulness in the solving of aesthetic problems, the know-how to combine and organize often disparate materials into a unified work. As Gide has said, "Every work of art is a problem solved."

Sometimes it will seem as if all the arts, during the past fifty years, had experienced premonitions, had sensed, amid the many disasters of our half-century, some vast final approaching catastrophe, and had striven feverishly to cram every resource, every experiment, innovation, and even every absurdity possible, into the brief interim remaining. Much of this experimentation, this reaching out for new ways and means, has resulted in genuine achievement. What is needed now, as that acute critic, the poet Louise Bogan, has said, is a lull in this revolutionary movement, an interlude during which to consolidate and perfect what has been gained, the new techniques, insights and aesthetic values that have been discovered. Will the time and the state of mind for this be granted? We must try to believe so, even when the signs and omens of the moment are not reassuring. The apocalypse with which the new religion of science has confronted us is singularly bleak and uninspiring—a Last Judgment, to be ushered in not by the sound of trumpets but by the screaming of sirens, and when that which shall be seen coming upon the clouds of heaven will have all of the fearsomeness and little of the tender glory described in the vision on Patmos.

◢§ 9

MAN'S STRUGGLE
TO UNDERSTAND

> *But of the tree of the knowledge of good and evil, thou shalt not eat of it: for in the day that thou eatest thereof thou shalt surely die.*
>
> GENESIS II:17

> *Knowledge is virtue.*
>
> SOCRATES

> *"Beauty is truth, truth beauty"—that is all Ye know on earth, and all ye need to know.*
>
> KEATS

> $E = mc^2$.
>
> EINSTEIN

◢§ Time and space, the basic components in our experience of what Einstein has called the space-time continuum, become, like everything else with which experience has continually to deal, so much a part of the act of experience itself as to be taken for granted. We are almost constantly under the practical necessity of coping with these phenomena and, for that very reason, are aware of them only on occasions. The arts offer some of these occasions. The plastic and pictorial arts, architecture, design, decoration, are, obviously, not only aware of space but in love with it. Music and literature, especially poetry, move with delight in the medium of time. If pattern, in the visual arts, serves to reveal spatial inter-relationships, rhythm functions in music and literature to create patterns in duration.

From the Einsteinian point of view, time can be regarded as an ingenious device for a further extension of three-dimensional space, making room, by means of change and succession, for a still larger number of possibilities. Almost everything that exists does so both in space and in time. This is true even of the spatial arts, of a painting, a statue, a building. Music and literature, on the other hand—apart from the physical forms that may serve as their depositories —exist in time only. The poem, for example, that you say over to yourself, the real poem, has no existence in space.*

* It is worth noting that what exists in time may or may not exist in space, but that what exists in space must exist in time also. The body of any literature, existing, like a physical body, in time (though, unlike it, outside of space), is, like a physical

Familiar and commonplace phenomena though they may be, time and space, like all the basic categories of experience, remain, however we may grope around them with logic, essentially unknowable. They are the prime mysteries in a universe where we are confronted with mystery at every turn. Bacon declared that "the subtlety of nature is greater, many times over, than the subtlety of the senses and understanding".** This is another way of saying that reality transcends the consciousness it includes. And here we have the key to the impulse behind scientific research. It is a response to the mystery that surrounds us. For as "the desire of the body is to continue, the deepest need of the mind is for order."*** The work of art, too, arises out of a need for the revelation of order in chaos, a need to make what is subjective objective, to understand and to share. It,

---

body, composed largely of what biologists term the "soma"—those cells that, subject to time and therefore perishing, eventually become the corpse. The "plasma", or seminal principle (to carry the analogy still further), will be represented by those few works that, by virtue of a special vitality inherent in them, are destined to escape, and thus to survive, the mortality of the rest. It is they who will generate, throughout time, by their creative energy and influence, the succession of works that constitute the continuing body of literature.

** Francis Bacon, *The Great Instauration*.

*** John Peale Bishop, "The Golden Bough", *The Collected Essays*, edited, and with an Introduction, by Edmund Wilson.

also, is, at root, a need for knowledge—knowledge
of experience itself as opposed to knowledge of the
objects of experience, to which science aspires. In a
world of mingled torment and delight, of beauty and
horror, arena of all these warring selves preying one
upon the other—caught in the endless flux and
mystery of things, himself in flux, himself con-
demned to preying upon others—man, a creature of
dreams and aspirations dragging the chain of his own
necessities, a spirit "fastened to a dying animal", has
tried, throughout the ages, by means of art and of
science, to fathom the situation in which he finds
himself, to bring some order, to make some sense,
out of his inner and outer environments.

Every age has been, for man, a difficult one, but
to some future historian, looking back from the vantage point of a happier era, it will perhaps be clear
that the age in which we are now living was, for
Western man, the most difficult age of all. The happy
and growing faith of the eighteenth-century Enlightenment, with its belief in natural goodness, in
human progress, and the perfectibility of life here
on earth, was badly shaken by the events of the
French Revolution and its long aftermath in the
Napoleonic wars. The nineteenth century's com-
parative peace and order, as well as the evolutionary
theories of Darwin, which it nourished, served to

revive the old confidence and hope, but in greatly diminished form, and after the global catastrophes that racked the better part of the first half of our own century, the faith born of the Enlightenment, while still smoldering in the popular mind, had largely burned itself out among the intellectuals and the intelligentsia. Faith in man, in progress, in the perfectibility of life here on earth, gave place, in many of the leading poets and writers, to disillusionment and despair. "Man is but a wretched creature", said T. E. Hulme,* the English philosopher, and Mr. Eliot wrote that "If you remove from the word 'human' all that the belief in the supernatural has given to man, you can view him finally as no more than an extremely clever, adaptable, and mischievous little animal".** A later form of reaction to the prevailing disillusionment is exemplified by existentialism, a philosophy that, abandoning all illusions about this world or hopes for a world to come, and regarding life here and now as a necessary evil, holds it desirable, nevertheless, to live life morally, and even with a certain nobility, since life is the human condition. This, of course, is the old Stoic or tragic view rehabilitated, and these two attitudes are re-

* T. E. Hulme, *Speculations.*
** T. S. Eliot, "Second Thoughts About Humanism", *Selected Essays of T. S. Eliot.*

flected in much of the poetry and the writing of our
time.

But Western man's confidence, his faith in himself and belief in his world, was to suffer, in our
century, a further setback, more crippling even than
that which had been inflicted upon it in two world
wars. By some tragic irony, man's supreme discovery
that matter and energy are mutually transformable
physical states, an achievement that placed him at
the threshold of a new age of almost unimaginable
possibilities for the enhancement of life, brought
with it, as its immediate consequence, the threat of
nuclear warfare and universal death. The day when
a cave-dweller first rubbed two sticks together and
discovered fire, fire that would burn the molecule,
had led to this ultimate discovery—a fire that would
burn the atom itself. Einstein's formula was proved to
have been prophetic, and man had laid his hand
upon the secret of things. Boundless energy, derived by unlocking the coiled fury of matter, was
to be his, for constructive purposes, once he had
learned how to harness it. Yet, in the interim, its
potential for annihilation threatened, because of his
emotional immaturity, instability, and aggressive-
ness, to wipe him, and perhaps all life, from the
planet. Once more the old problem of evil confronted man but, this time, in a form more appalling

than the form in which it had confronted Job.
Human beings, from the beginning, even as Job,
have been hard put to it to reconcile the idea of evil
with the idea of a beneficent Creator. Our conception of evil, from Job's day onward, has almost
always been anthropocentric. Evil, according to this
conception, is whatever is uncomfortable for man.
It seems seldom to have occurred to the writers and
poets of our time—Robinson Jeffers was a notable
exception—that there may be interests higher than
those of man.*

All in all, the first half of the twentieth century,
in spite of its amazing scientific and technological
achievements, the extraordinary power it has given

---

* Perhaps, in defining what is evil, we should apply Einstein's
relativity theory, and distinguish (taking a hint from Bacon)
"the thing-in-reference-to-man from the thing-in-reference-to-
the-universe" (Francis Bacon, *The Great Instauration*). There
might be a difference there. Just as the simultaneity or non-
simultaneity of two events widely separated in space can be
experienced only by Omnipresence, so what is good and what
is evil can be determined only by Omniscience. And it could
do no harm to apply the relativity theory to literary values also,
regarding each critic as a separate system of reference. This
would help, on the one hand, to take the sting out of Mr.
Ciardi's condemnation of all of Whittier, except for 16 lines—
or was it 14½?—and, on the other, from Mr. Shapiro's whole-
sale indictment of most contemporary poetry. (See the account
of Mr. Ciardi's speech at Washington University, October 7,
1959, reported by *American Poetry Publishers*, Nov.–Dec. 1959
issue, and Mr. Shapiro's article, "What's the Matter with
Poetry?" in *The New York Times Book Review*, December 13,
1959.)

man over things, finds him more downcast, less sure
of himself and of the world around him, and more
disillusioned, than in any other era that we know
anything about. His anxiety and dejection consort
strangely with his triumphs in the fields of science
and industry, with the enormous hopes and opportunities offered by that future world to which his
talents have now given him the key. Too much has
happened too fast in our century, and we have been
bewildered and frightened by what we, ourselves,
have brought about.

It is easy to lose faith in man, in progress, in the
possibilities of human life here on earth, and it has
never been easier than during the period that Mr.
Auden has characterized as "The Age of Anxiety".
The disillusionment and despair, as well as the
apathy, so prevalent in our time, find frequent expression in the poetry of the period: directly, in a
cynical pessimism or, indirectly, in the embracing
of doctrines of transcendence that write off the world
and life of here and now, and transfer ultimate value
to a realm beyond and above them. And these expressions have validity and are important, not only
as an indication of our concern and discontent with
things as they are, but because they represent a continuing effort, through one of the arts, to understand
what we are experiencing.

Yet a change must come. Man cannot survive without belief in himself or faith in the potentialities of life. The factors undermining these normal attitudes have been with us for a long time. They have, we must hope, reached their maximum at this hour of crisis. And in looking at man and measuring his progress, or the absence of it, we must survey larger spans of time than those represented by a few centuries. Progress may be slow, but there has been progress. Twentieth-century man stands higher than the Stone Age man, not merely in the extension of his physical powers through scientific and technological devices; intellectually and spiritually he has come a long way from his primitive ancestors. Moreover, his potentialities have not yet begun to be developed. What are a hundred thousand years, in terms of evolution!

We are faced today with a challenge so immediate, so overwhelming, as to contain, paradoxically, an element of hope. A creature considerably lower than the angels has been endowed by science with extensions of his body that enable him to hurl an object around the sun or to wipe out the life of a continent with his left hand. If he cannot grow great enough in spirit to match the greatness of his newly acquired physical and intellectual powers, he will perish from the earth. May not the mortal urgency of the challenge force him to by-pass the process of evolution, to take on now the moral stature required for survival? Will not the law of survival itself compel men to become at last the brothers they truly are? In that case, having given up nothing worth having, reconciled, almost as if reborn, we may enter a true Golden Age, a world and a future as superior to the present-day world as is the present-day world to that of the anthropoid ape. War will have given place to a world community, and progress will continue as much along spiritual as along material lines. The fostering, the cherishing, the enrichment of life, on a crowded planet, will demand not only the utmost in material resources that science can wring from the secrets of matter, it will demand also the transcendence of self to an extreme degree, in every individual, and in ever-increasing measure.

The nature of things, from the human point of view, is tragic. To live and to die calls for all the nobility man can muster. Through art and through science he will continue his tireless, age-long quest for knowledge—knowledge of the world of experience, knowledge of the structure of things. He may, within certain limits, conquer space and visit other worlds. It is conceivable that he will be able to establish communication with intelligent beings on distant planets, beings more advanced, perhaps, than himself, more experienced in dealing with the predicament of life, more expert in probing the mysteries of reality. With them he can compare notes; from them he can learn invaluable things. His long solitude in the universe will have been broken. But the fate of life, in the individual and in the race, will remain unchanged. The ultimate mystery will remain unchanged. And so long as man lives surrounded by mystery, so long as reality transcends the consciousness it includes, so long will he strive, by all the means at his disposal, to discover or to create some meaningful order out of the seeming chaos that confronts him. Goethe said a significant thing when he remarked that he who has neither art nor science must have religion.

◆§ Index

[127]